DORKING IN WARTIME

A diary of events compiled chiefly from the Dorking Advertiser
and from various other sources.

by

David Knight

Published by DAVID KNIGHT
Furlong Road, Westcott, Dorking, Surrey.
and printed by Rayment Printers Limited
5 Horsham Road, Dorking, Surrey.

ISBN 0 9515328 0 4

The Dorking A.R.P. map can be seen at Dorking Museum

FRONT COVER:
L.D.V. Parade on the Nower, July 1940 — see page 24

INTRODUCTION

David Knight captures the grim reality of wartime Dorking with his diary of events carefully compiled from official records, Dorking Advertiser archives and personal accounts.

He uses a vast amount of material to link events covering the period from 1938 to 1946, vividly illustrating Dorking through the hostilities.

Momentous events are brought alive through the experience of individuals and are effortlessly bound together to make compulsive reading.

Although the town entered calmly enough into war conditions without panic or alarm, the harsh reality of those times soon became apparent when the skies filled with aircraft and trainloads of soldiers snatched from the beaches of Dunkirk passed through the town in June, 1940.

The illustrations of wartime Dorking are unique.

Apart from the vivid historical record, David Knight includes little related incidents. For instance, the town's great composer, Dr. Ralph Vaughan Williams, was among those who responded to a call for sandbag fillers . . .

Readers will be interested in detailed accounts of the many bombs which fell on the district and the number of aircraft brought down.

David Knight handles the huge volume of material with meticulous care to provide a fascinating account of the town's war years.

For countless people it will bring back memories . . . some fond, some grim.

Greta Morley
Editor, Dorking Advertiser

ACKNOWLEDGEMENTS

I would like to thank firstly the Dorking Advertiser and its former Editor, Alfred de Araujo, for kindly allowing me to go through back numbers of the Advertiser and to extract and reproduce much of the material seen here. Without the generous help of the Advertiser and its splendid staff, this book could not have been produced. My thanks are due in addition to the new Editor, Greta Morley, who has continued this cooperation and very kindly agreed to write an introduction.

I had considerable help too from the Deutsche Dienststelle in Berlin, Dorking Museum, the Public Record Office at Kew, the Surrey and Sussex Aviation Society and the West Sussex County Times.

I am grateful to the following people for their help in various ways: Miss Audrey Aitken, Mrs Margaret Black, Margaret Chennell, Mr Reginald Chilvers, Miss P Cooke, the late Frank Coombes, John Coombes, Mrs RM Eileen Crowder, Ruth Dyson, Steve Fletcher, Keith Harding of Goodness Gracious Photography and Design, Marion Herridge, Miss Margaret Horne, my wife Joy, my dear late mother Ethel Knight, Peter Knight, the late Miss Phyllis Kynaston, Michael Levy, Clare and Archie McMillan, my two very dear friends 'Pip' and John Mee, Doris Mercer, Edith Mercer, Mrs Marie Miller, J A Milne, Richard Raspin, Joe Richardson, Reg Rose, Kim and Colin Sanderson, Angela and Iain Sanderson, Julius Schurgers, Miss Kathleen Spooner, Mrs Pam Toler of the WRVS, Georg Trunsperger, JEN Walker, Mr Arthur Wetherell and Mrs Nellie White.

David Knight
Westcott, September 1989.

For abbreviations see back page.

The Dorking Advertiser reports:

January 14/38 Vicar of St. Paul's church, the Rev. A.C. Nickol, suggests bomb tube shelter through town.

June 10/38 Dorking British Legion compiling a census of Dorking's requirements of anti-gas respirators.

June 17/38 Westcott. A public meeting in connection with A.R.P. arrangements, by the Westcott British Legion Branch.

June 24/38 Westcott. Listeners at the above meeting wanted for voluntary training as wardens for dealing with mustard gas, incendiary bombs etc.

June 24/38 Respirators will be issued free.

July 22/38 The old Post Office in South Street will open next week for use as a fitting centre for civilian respirators.

January 20/39 Apparatus for air raid precautions in Dorking and for A.R.P. training is slowly but surely being assembled. The latest arrival is a gas chamber. This is for the purpose of giving men and women the experience of being in gas- while wearing gas masks of course. Seventy-five volunteers went into the gas chamber last Sunday morning. In future, a visit to the gas chamber will be part of the training course. Tear gas is used in the chamber.

January 20-27/39 Evacuation schemes going ahead.

February 3/39 War shelters urged for Dorking. Rev. A.C. Nickol of St. Paul's said "If war comes, which God forbid, what provision have the authorities made for the safety of the inhabitants of Dorking? We have been provided with gas masks, but gas masks will not protect us from fire, blast, splinters, falling debris or the demolition of buildings. It should be remembered that during the crisis of last September, people fled to Dorking from London, filling up every house. In addition large numbers of children were brought to our town."

Still going on about the underground shelter in the town.

February 3/39 Anti-gas lectures at Westcott. The cost was estimated at £6, comprising hire of hall at 7s.6d per night on one night a week for eight weeks and payment to lecturer of 7s.6d. per lecture.

April 7/39 A section of the Dorking public has been urging that bomb proof shelters should be constructed in or near the town. Some suggested that tunnels should be pierced into the hillside of Cotmandene and the Nower, while others think that the caves near High Street should be converted into shelters. The

Government advised by experts and having full knowledge of the likelihood of bombs and of the possibilities of protection, have not given support to the construction of deep shelters.

<u>April 28/39</u> Certain rooms on the lower ground floor of the old Court House and Police Station, Dorking, are to be used for the purpose of a control centre for county A.R.P. services in time of war.

<u>May 5/39</u> On the alert next Monday. The general public are asked to cooperate in the test by remaining indoors or in their gardens during the period mentioned. Those whose duties necessitate their leaving their houses are urged to take their civilian respirators with them.

<u>May 5/39</u> Ambulance drivers appointed. Sir - The Dorking Urban Council, who should be model employers, are not I think, offering fair wages in advertising for a driver-mechanic for the ambulance and fire brigade service at £2.15s. per week. The man who gets the job will have three qualifications. He will be a motor mechanic and driver; he will be a first aid man (the advertisement requires that applicants should possess first aid certificates), and he will be a fireman. All that for £2.15s. per week! Well, its not generous.
Yours etc; B. Baker, Westcott.

<u>May 5/39</u> Mont-Smiths are so convinced that war is not imminent that they agree to refund all moneys paid for suits ordered now if this country is at war in Europe within two months, and all such suits will be given free of charge. Dated April 28th 1939.

The surest and safest means of transport is the bicycle. That is why A.R.P. Wardens are instructed to use cycles. Think it over - no tax, no petrol, no bother at all, and Currys offer you the pick of British cycles for as little as 1s. 6d. weekly or cash prices from £3 5s. - call at 208, High Street, Dorking and talk it over with the Manager.

<u>May 12/39</u> A.R.P. Mobilisation. On Monday evening Dorking had the excitement of an A.R.P. test mobilisation. At least, it was an excitement in some respects, in others it was not. The enemy did not cause many incidents.

The mobilisation covered South-Eastern area of Surrey - the Borough of Reigate, the Caterham and Warlingham Urban District, the Dorking Urban District, the Dorking and Horley Rural District, and the Godstone Rural District - and it was arranged primarily by the Area Director of Operations. The Dorking district came into the presumed air raid, but not to a large extent, and therefore the A.R.P. services had little to do. Some, chiefly the A.R.P volunteers in the rural areas had almost nothing to do.

Warning of enemy aircraft approaching was given at 8 p.m. It had been intended that a fleet of bombing planes should fly over, but a message was received five minutes before the exercise was due to begin that aircraft were not available.

Within fifteen minutes of the sounding of the sirens the report centre knew that all services throughout the urban area were prepared for action. That was a good performance.

After the warning and the manning of the posts, the first duties fell upon the wardens. Equipped with whistles, rattles or handbells, they patrolled their areas warning the public that an air raid was taking place, and looking for incidents that required the services of the A.R.P. squads. Methods of indicating incidents had been pre-arranged. A circle of yellow powder and yellow smoke bomb for mustard gas, yellow powder and white flour and white smoke bomb for ordinary poison gas, white powder circle representing the extent of a crater caused by H.E. bombs, and red ochre and thermite bomb for incendiary bombs. The air raid wardens had to look out for these indications.

The first incident reported by wardens was that a high explosive bomb had fallen on the Punchbowl Hotel, in Reigate Road, that there were four casualties there, and that the hotel was on fire. A stretcher party and an ambulance party were called from their posts at the Fire and Ambulance Station, West Street. With one of the ambulances they went to the Punchbowl, where they found casualties (Boy Scouts) each holding an envelope containing a statement of the nature of the supposed injuries. The stretcher party (dressed rather uncomfortably in light anti-gas clothing) rendered first aid, and the ambulance party took the casualties to the first aid post in the Council Chamber at Pippbrook.

The news that the Punchbowl Hotel was on fire did not reach the Fire Station as promptly as it should have done. In the rush of messages to the various squads, the message to the Fire Brigade was forgotten. The human element failed. However, eventually (when probably the hotel would have been burnt to the ground), the news reached the Fire Station, and a crew of auxiliary firemen, with a trailer-pump towed by a car and a lorry carrying further fire - fighting equipment, rushed to the fire. Quickly, in the awkward circumstances, they got two jets of water playing on the burning hotel. Well, not exactly on the burning building, because it was not burning, but actually on the gardens at the side. Still, the water was there if the fire had been there!

The bomb falling on the Punchbowl Hotel also caused a blocking of the main road, and accordingly the road repair squad was called. But the road obstruction was marked only by a chalk line. A party of hefty Council roadmen (who formed the road repair squad) could not do much with a chalk line. After turning out promptly with shovels and other equipment for dealing with a big hole in the road, they looked disgustedly for a while at the chalk mark, reported that they had cleared the obstruction, and went to deal with another incident.

This was a more elaborately staged incident, arranged by the

7

moment. Whilst these casualties were being bandaged, lifted on to stretchers and transported to the Hut, two more bombs fell. One at the junction of Westcott Street and Balchins Lane, where another bridge "went West", and the other up at the Hildens road, where live the people who look down on the rest of the village.

But the knock-out blow occurred at 9.30, when H.E. blew up the Hut and part, at least of the mobile unit, which at once commenced to rescue patients from the debris. During this dreadful task a phosgene gas bomb fell in St. John's Road, where the warden on duty twirled his rattle vigorously. The warden downwind took up the alarm, but the mobile unit personnel, except for one member, appparently did not hear the latter rattle and therefore were gassed. In fact, the evening was from a training point of view a great success!

The bombing party Mr. H.R. Bourne and Lieut. L. Horne, tried various methods of eluding the vigilance of the wardens. Before lighting a bomb they looked both ways and round corners and over hedges to see if a warden was in sight. But in every case except one, the warden concerned won, and within 30 seconds was on the spot writing out his or her report before running to the nearest telephone. The isolated case happened when the warden on Coast Hill was patrolling near the top instead of the bottom as the bomb exploded. After all, even a warden cannot be in two places at once; but his time was only two and a half minutes. In fact, the wardens of the village seemed to wear seven - league boots and possessed eyes like hawks. Lucky Westcott!"

<u>July 28/39</u> Milton Court has been acquired by a big business concern for emergency offices in case of war.

<u>August 4/39</u> Following the Home Office announcement that during August supplies of the special respirators for small children, and of the anti-gas helmets for babies, will begin to become available, arrangements are being made to learn the numbers of these articles required in this district. A census of all children under the age of four and a half years will be taken by the air raid wardens, and will be kept up-to-date with additions through births and deletions through children reaching the age limit. The respirators and helmets will not be distributed to the houses where there are children until war comes.

<u>September 8/39</u> The Evacuation, Dorking receives London guests. The evacuation of over 3000 mothers and children from London into Dorking district last weekend was carried through wonderfully well in the circumstances.

The first train load arrived at 11.40 a.m. on Friday. The evacuees were about 500 East Dulwich schoolchildren, with their teachers. They were taken by buses to the Dorking Halls where orderly arrangements had been made so that the children passed rapidly and without confusion through the various essential channels - first, to medical inspection; then to the department where rations for 48 hours were given to each child; next to the

10

registration department and lastly into the care of billeting officers, who took parties out to the pre-arranged billets. These arrangements worked with a smoothness which was thrilling - "like the wheels of a well-oiled machine", said someone who was there.

By 1.35 p.m all the evacuated children in the first party had left the Dorking Halls, and were safely and satisfactorily in their new temporary homes. Similarly, a second train load of school children who arrived at Dorking at 2.40 p.m. were dealt with by 3.40 p.m. With the organisation now running perfectly, Dorking was ready to receive further parties of school children.

But, on Saturday, a much more difficult job presented itself. That afternoon a train load of mothers with young children arrived. Here it was not so easy to arrange billets satisfactory to all parties. When, on Sunday, two more train loads of mothers with young children arrived, the work became really difficult.

The chief trouble was to find billets in which mothers with two, three or even more young children could be accommodated. The mothers refused to allow their families to be split up in two or more billets, even though in the same road. And there are not many houses in this district which can provide accommodation at short notice for a big family. Some compulsory billeting had to be done, and some of the evacuated families elected to return to their homes. Since Sunday, many readjustments have been made. That re-shuffling of evacuees into billets which more satisfactorily suit the personal convenience of the householders and their guests is still going on. It is work demanding tact and much patience.

Those however, are minor troubles, due chiefly to the fact that the London authorities sent to Dorking many more mothers with young children and many fewer unaccompanied schoolchildren than were expected. Thus it happens that numerous billets in Dorking reserved for unaccompanied schoolchildren have not been taken yet. Dorking acted as the reception centre for the part of rural areas around Dorking as well as for the town itself, and most of the evacuees in the first parties went to the villages.

Still, whatever little troubles have arisen, they were not the fault of the Dorking evacuation organisation. Working under Mrs. Lindsay's leadership, the members of the W.V.S. did their noble work magnificently, and many women who were not originally in that organisation assisted. Some men helped too, chiefly in transport work and as billeting officers. Most of the voluntary workers were hard at it for very long hours each day. Some, did not have a real meal at a table for four days and scarcely any sleep.

As the subject is evacuation, I move ahead six months and give a couple of extracts from "Dulwich Central School Magazine, Westcott. A record of Evacuation to Westcott, September 1939 - Easter 1940."

First a letter from the headmaster of Dulwich Central School:
"It is with a certain amount of pride that I write a note of introduction to this record of our first few months away from London. With mixed feelings on that memorable first of September we stepped out of our London daily round into the unknown of the English countryside. How we have since fared you will be able to judge from this record of our impressions. You will read of the friends we have made, of the sights and sounds of the countryside which have become full of meaning to us, and of the score and one ways in which we have found interests.

When the welcome day for our return to Dulwich comes, we shall, I am quite certain, part from our numerous friends in Westcott with sincere regret. At the same time we shall take back to London a genuine appreciation of many of the problems of our country neighbours, as well as some insight into their surroundings and their interests. On behalf of staff, pupils and myself, I should like to express our deep appreciation to our Westcott friends of their hospitality and of their real and successful efforts to help us through, what has certainly been the most disturbed period in the history of London Education.
March 1940   James Pipe"

Secondly, one of the many letters written by the pupils:

"Our Journey to Westcott"

"All children to attend school tomorrow" was one of the headlines of the newspapers on Monday August 21st, and underneath was a list of the clothes we had to take with us. Though it meant the end of the summer holiday, most children turned up promptly at school the next day. Mr. Pipe explained our being recalled and we spent the rest of the day playing various kinds of games. For the next week or so we went to school each day to await the time for evacuation. Mr. Weeks and Mr. Miller took us for organised games in the park, and we were entertained by a band composed of Robson, Baker, Mr. Davis and mandolin player John Corner. The radio was turned on every hour or so to hear the news bulletins, and the tension was increased when the news came that schools in nearby boroughs were being evacuated. On Friday September 1st, it happened. We marched from school to East Dulwich Station, without any fuss, as we had had several practices previously, a few of the boys going ahead with the hand cart, which they managed to tip over on the way, containing the luggage. As we marched through the streets, being subjected to much staring from the passers-by, we laughed and joked. Some of us were greatly puzzled as to where our destination would be. We waited for about a quarter of an hour on the platform before the train came in, and then climbed in, making sure to be in the same compartment as our friends.

During practically the whole journey, our compartment resounded to our boisterous singing as we did our best to keep in tune with John Corner's mandolin.

12

When the train squealed to a halt there was a rush for the windows, to see where the journey had ended, and as most of us had thoughts that we were going to a place somewhere in the area of Chichester, we were greatly astonished to find that the name of the station was Dorking North. Then pulling our luggage down from the racks, we jumped out.

As we walked out of the station we were confronted by a long line of ominbuses, which we presumed were to be our next means of conveyance, and we were right. They took us to "Dorking Halls", where we were examined by a doctor and given enough food for forty eight hours. Going out through a side door we stepped into a small single-decker bus, which took us through Dorking, and along the now well-known Dorking road to Westcott. There, we were herded into a small hall which we afterwards found out to be the Reading Room. I did not have long to wait before a pleasant, elderly lady came along and asked for three boys. At once, one of my friends suggested my two brothers and myself, and we were accepted. Our foster-mother-to-be then took us across Westcott Green and down Westcott Street, where we were greeted by her dog, Angus. As we continued, we introduced ourselves and talked about the evacuation. Our short walk ended at our billet, where we found a hearty meal and a friend waiting for us.
James Smith".

I now move back six months to the "Dorking Advertiser"

September 8/39   Those who are old enough to remember the outbreak of the Great War in 1914 - and they need not be very old - cannot fail to have been struck by the enormous differences between conditions then and conditions today.

Dorking entered calmly enough into war conditions last weekend, and there was no signs of panic or undue alarm. Even that first false air raid alarm, within half an hour of the outbreak of war, did not cause violent excitement. There was great activity of course, among A.R.P. workers, ready at their posts. Most of the general public hurried to their homes without being ordered to do so. The A.R.P report centres received warning of another presumed air attack in the early hours of Monday morning, but in this case the approaching aircraft was known to be not in this vicinity and no general alarm was given in the Dorking district, although it was given in other areas, including some parts of Surrey. However, in this instance again as on Sunday morning, the aircraft which had caused the alarm were quickly identified as friendly. Thus, Dorking has passed fairly smoothly into the unknown and troublesome days of war. Then, early on Wednesday morning, the warning sirens sounded again, and the A.R.P. personnel were on the alert for over two hours, while the public remained mainly in their homes.

Dorking has become very crowded during the past few days. Not only has there been the big influx of evacuated children with their mothers and teachers from London, but also London firms, who have taken premises in this district as emergency offices, have sent down their staffs of clerks and added to the population. The High Street particularly has seemed exceptionally busy these last few days during daylight, due of course to the evacuees being out a good deal and also to the fact that the schools are closed. The elementary schoolchildren should have returned last Monday, but an announcement has been made that the schools will be temporarily closed. The evacuation and billeting officers, with their keen staffs of voluntary workers, have been very busy (and probably very warm in the glorious summer weather) and they have now completed their main job satisfactorily. Places of entertainment and amusement were ordered to close on Sunday until further notice, and the last performances at the Dorking cinemas for a while were given on Saturday evening. An Army Recruiting Office is being opened in the New Parade.

Last week, the total of Auxiliary Firemen enrolled at the Dorking Fire Station was 50. By Monday evening this week the total had swollen to nearly 150. Recruits have been rolling in almost too rapidly, as they cannot be trained in a few hours. The members of the regular Fire Brigade are on full time duty, and so too are some of the Auxiliary Firemen, some stretcher bearers, Special Constables, and others of the A.R.P. personnel. Most of the A.R.P. volunteers are working in shifts. Dorking's "blackout" appears to be very complete, and the householders seem to have co-operated particularly well in preventing any lights in their houses being visible from outside.

September 29/39 Mr. T.M. Ward, Dorking's A.R.P. officer, has sent us the following extract from a letter received from the Home Office: "The Home Office have been asked whether pedestrians are allowed to go on their way when the air raid warning has sounded. The warning time before the enemy planes are likely to be within bombing range is five to seven minutes. A pedestrian can go on his way at his own risk, but for his own sake, and for the sake of those who may have to look after him, he should not do so unless he can get to his home or his work in a matter of minutes, without running. If he is within a few minutes of his destination, he can properly try to get there, otherwise he should go to the nearest shelter as directed by the wardens or police."

October 6/39 The Dorking schools are reopening but under war-time conditions with limited numbers in each class. The following particulars of what is happening at North Holmwood are typical of what is being done generally. The evacuated children, with their own teachers , occupy the school buildings for three hours in the morning and spend two hours in the afternoon in out-of-school activities. The North Holmwood children, with many unofficial evacuated children, work the reverse shift and, despite, or because of, a drastic change in the normal curriculum, it is apparent that the children are settling down to reasonably serious work. The Village Hall is used for activities such as country dancing, music, dramatic work, needlework,

14

physical training etc, and the Boys' Club holds two shifts of 80 very happy infants.

November 10/39 Food Rationing, books issued in Dorking. All consumers in the Dorking urban area should have received their ration books by now. Although coupons are available for butcher's meat and cooking fats, the only commodities to be rationed in the first instance are butter, bacon and ham.

Supplies of sugar are ample to meet normal requirements, and the rationing of sugar might be postponed indefinitely if consumers restrict their purchases to 1 lb. per head per week.

November 10/39 Lamp-posts in the black-out. The Council of the Dorking and District Chamber of Commerce resolved at a meeting on Tuesday evening, to suggest to the Dorking Urban District Council that lamp posts in dangerous positions should be painted with luminous paint, or alternatively, with white paint for 5 ft. from the ground so as to make them more visible during black-out hours. It was stated that several cases had occurred of persons walking into lamp posts in the dark and suffering severe injuries.

December 1/39 Dorking Council. The Fire Brigade Committee reported that Mr. B.T. Pearce, of Pasture Wood Riding School, Abinger,a member of the A.F.S., had lent without charge to the Council a Rolls-Royce car for use as an auxiliary tender. The loan was accepted with thanks to Mr. Pearce.

                    *   *   *

January 5/40 Alice B... of Roselawn, Guildford Road, Westcott, was alleged to have left a scullery door open, thus allowing a light to be seen outside - case dismissed with a warning.

January 5/40 To the Fire Brigade and Ambulance Committee, the Chief Officer reported that the Rolls-Royce car which had been loaned to the Council had been altered and adapted for auxiliary service at a cost of about £4.10s. The Committee congratulated the auxiliary firemen on the way they had done this work.

January 5/40 The A.R.P. reported that Messrs. Henleys, Milton Court, Westcott, had established a wardens' post. It was resolved that this be recognised as an official post.

Continued from "The Henley Telegraph" Vol.VIII Emergency Issue 1939 - No.59.

"Milton Court A.R.P. At Milton Court full provision has been made against air raid eventualities. In positions effectively screened by trees, eight trenches have been prepared and camouflaged.

Every member of the staff at Milton Court has been allotted a place in a trench; and those working in the upper storey, who have furthest to go, occupy the trenches nearest to the main building. To save confusion when evacuating the building, the departments have a set route so as to make the best possible use of the two staircases. Each trench is in charge of a trench leader who is supplied with an emergency lantern for shepherding his charges in and out of the trench should the alarm sound at night time, and it is his job to make a list of those people allocated to his trench so that every member of the staff can be accounted for.

A rota of air raid wardens becomes operative on the receipt of a warning and these in turn keep in touch with the head warden's post in the main building. The first aid squad, qualified first aiders, stand to with all the necessary equipment to deal with accidents.

Fire risks are being covered in the building by stirrup pumps at strategic positions; and the Company has just bought an Apex "500" trailer fire pump. A fire station is being built on the lakeside, and a sump dug below water level which will give the pump almost unlimited water. The two lakes at Milton Court are fed by a stream, which, controlled by a system of sluices can give all the water necessary for efficient fire fighting. Two complete crews of firemen are being trained by experts."

The first A.R.P. Officer was Mr. G.I. Scott.

January 5/40 The Surveyor reported to the A.R.P. Commmittee that considerable damage was being done by children to the sandbagged wardens' posts and other buildings. The A.R.P. Committee decided to write to all head teachers in the district asking them to talk to the children about this damage and to endeavour to prevent its recurrence.

The A.R.P. Committee were informed that Councillor Somner and the A.R.P. Officer had attended a course at Reading in incendiary bomb control and were now qualified instructors.

Mr. Bell asked whether "the ridiculous shovels and sand buckets that were dished out for dealing with incendiary bombs" had any value. "I am terribly sceptical", he added.

Mr. Somner replied that the method was now of secondary importance. A much cheaper and more officient method had been devised with stirrup pumps.

January 5/40 Until this week, few, if any Dorking people knew that there was a British ship carrying the local name of "Box Hill". Unhappily, this week has brought the news that S.S. "Box Hill" has gone to the bottom of the North Sea. On Sunday, the "Box Hill", a vessel of 5600 tons, steaming somewhere in the North Sea, sank two or three minutes after an explosion caused by enemy action, and it is feared that 20 of her crew of 32 have perished.

February 2/40 Dorking Council. Two cars for £26. The Chairman of the A.R.P. Committee reported to the Finance Committee that, as directed, he and the Surveyor had bought an Armstrong Siddeley car and an Austin car for use as stretcher party cars at a total cost of £26 that being £4 less than the figure authorised by the Committee.

March 1/40   Five hundred and fifty "baby protective helmets" - the official name for the queer contraptions in which infants can be protected from the horrors of poison gas - have been received for the use of the babies of the Dorking Urban District. They are being distributed to the parents of babies under the age of two years. The helmets are expensive articles and it is vitally important that great care should be taken not to damage them. They are Government property - when the child reaches the age of two years, its helmet should be exchanged for a respirator suitable for a child of that age.

March 29/40   Readers are reminded of the test of the air raid warning siren which is made on the first Wednesday of every month.

April 26/40   Among 400 babies' anti-gas helmets returned to the authorities, the following articles were found inside the helmets: Breadcrumbs, sticky sweets, pieces of paper, playing cards, wooden pegs, a drinking glass, a civilian respirator, bus tickets, partly eaten cooked meat, and postcards. That news is given in a circular letter, issued from the Dorking A.R.P. headquarters, together with details of defects caused to helmets chiefly through carelessness among parents to whom the helmets have been issued. It seems to be necessary to stress again the importance of taking great care of these expensive helmets.

May 24/40   In the Dorking Police Division over 1400 men have offered their services for the Local Defence Volunteers. The Volunteers will begin regular duties this weekend; some have already been on duty unofficially. For Dorking and the immediate neighbourhood there are 500 volunteers. Of these, 234 are being called for immediate duties. These men are ex-servicemen not under 40 years of age, who have had training. The other volunteers will be called for training and duty in the near future. Mr. J.F. Somner and Mr. H.M. Gordon Clark are organising the local volunteers. A meeting is to be held this evening to approve arrangements already made and to set the local defence machinery into immediate operation. Some uniforms and rifles have been received for the Dorking volunteers. Mr. S.C. Fuller is acting as armourer in charge of the rifles. The volunteers'headquarters will be over the Fire Station.

May 24/40   On Sunday morning, people in and around Dorking saw, over the Ranmore hills, something slowly descending from the sky. It looked from a distance like a parachute. People thought for a moment that a German invasion with parachute troops had begun and they shouted to their neighbours. But a British aeroplane was circling near the falling object and, if it was an enemy parachute, it was landing only one enemy soldier in a remote rural district, so the danger did not appear to be alarming.

Nevertheless many people took steps to acquaint the authorities with what they had seen. Some went to the police station; others phoned there. There were, indeed, so many phone calls to the police that the telephone exchange had to be told not to put further calls through to the station but to tell the anxious people that the object they had seen was not a parachute but a barrage balloon which had broken loose. While the balloon had been over Leatherhead, an aeroplane gunner had riddled it with bullets to cause it to deflate and descend. It came to earth in the neighbourhood of Polesden Lacey. Another truant barrage balloon came over the Dorking district, also on Sunday. This one came down near Broome Hall, Coldharbour, after being riddled with bullets from a R.A.F. fighter.

May 31/40 Dorking Council. The Fire Brigade Committee were authorised to spend £60 in buying two or three vehicles as tenders for auxiliary fire pumps.

When the Council reached this part of the reports, the clerk announced that a 38 h.p. Buick car had been given to the Council by Mr. R.A. Fulford, of The Cottage, Punchbowl Lane, and that a 20 h.p. Chrysler car had been loaned for the duration of the war by Mr. R.F. Colam, K.C. These cars would be used as fire tenders.

May 31/40 A minor criticism which has been heard about the Local Defence Volunteers in Dorking is that some of the volunteers are already engaged in important A.R.P. organisation. We find that criticism is not justified. The few men now serving in both organisations are only temporarily doing duty with the L.D.V., acting as instructors, and preliminary organisers because of special qualifications. They are not neglecting their A.R.P.duties and, were an air raid to occur, they would devote themselves solely to A.R.P. work.

May 31/40 Contrary to the many rumours circulating in Dorking, no one from Dorking apart from enemy aliens has been interned. That statement has been given to us authoritatively by Police Superintendant Hilton, who is anxious (as are all decent people) that the circulation of these rumours should cease. If the practice of repeating rumours and idle gossip continues, there will come a time when an offender will be brought before a court and severely punished.

May 31/40 Mrs. Lloyd, of Hartsfield, Betchworth has kindly loaned to Dorking Toc H the use of the rooms over the Milk Bar at 116 High Street, Dorking, and the Toc H men are now busy devoting their spare time to preparing the premises as a canteen with reading, writing and games rooms for men in the Services. The premises were, until a few years ago used as the Dorking Club. Therefore they admirably arranged structurally for club purposes. There are two big rooms, a large hall which in Dorking Club days, accommodated billiards tables, a bar (which will become a canteen counter) and cloakrooms. An additional advantage is that the premises are in the centre of the town, where they can be readily

Train with Dunkirk survivors passing through Westcott, June 2 1940. Passing out slips of paper with their names and addresses. See page 21

One of the American cars used as a fire tender. See page 18

found by the Servicemen who are strangers in the district. The premises will be opened as soon as possible, but there is a great deal of work to be done before they are ready. Toc H men, with their usual happy willingness to undertake any manual labour for

On the right — Mr. G. I. Scott with assistant at Milton Court.   *See page 16*

a good cause, have "taken their coats off" to the big job of cleaning and fitting the rooms.

Toc H have been opening their headquarters near the Chart lane Institute, as a club for Servicemen, but those premises have to be vacated soon.

June 7/40 The people living near a certain Surrey station (Redhill) are not likely to forget, for many years to come, the scenes that have been enacted within their sight and hearing during this last memorable week. Somehow those trainloads of tired but courageous soldiers, snatched by a miracle from the hell of Dunkirk, brought home the realities of war more vividly than anything we have read in the newspapers. I think too, that the soldiers for their part are not likely to forget the welcome, the utmost care that willing hands could give them, that they received on the platforms of that station in the short time while that their trains halted there. All that is best in human nature came to the surface on these occasions.

This next brief account is from "A Footplateman Remembers the Southern" by Jim Rowe an engine fireman of one of the engines: "Most of the time the troops were in a bad way, many with just a blanket to cover themselves, but there was only one thing they ever asked of us and that was to notify someone that they were safe. I collected many pieces of paper from them with just a name, address and signature, and the driver I was with agreed to share them and post a note to each addresss, together with a note of our own, explaining that they were safe in this country".

June 14/40 The efforts of those who assisted at the canteen at the railway station in Surrey with so much zeal and energy are still held in grateful remembrance by the troops of the B.E.F., on their evacuation from Dunkirk, to whom this kindly service was so willingly rendered. The canteens were organised at a moment's notice directly the need was known. A correspondent writes: "It was inspiring to note how, with one accord, all communities responded to the call for help - many in hard work, in gifts of food, and in helping with the funds to purchase all that was required. The generosity and the eagerness of all has never been felt so strongly in the locality, a fact which is most encouraging under present difficult conditions. Day and night this work was carried on by willing helpers who had to adapt themselves to contingencies at a moments notice. To mention any persons or groups individually would be too big an undertaking, but all must have felt well rewarded by the appreciation and thanks shown by our troops and by parents who have since written".

June 21/40 The Toc H Services Club, over the Golden Milk Bar in Dorking High Street is now open each evening, and it will soon grow in popularity as it becomes more and more known among Servicemen. It is pleasantly furnished and well equipped with books, magazines, writing materials, a canteen and games - excepting for the one much demanded game of billiards. Is there

21

a billiards table available as a loan or gift to the Club?

June 21/40   The disappearance of familiar signposts in the district is a sign of the times we live in, an indication of the grim facts up to which our island home is facing.   But the removal of signposts as a means of making an invader's task more difficult is not enough and the Home Secretary has made an Order under the Defence Regulations, prohibiting the display of any sign, including any direction post, place-name or map, which furnishes any indication of the name of, the situation of, the direction of, or the distance to any place, if it can be seen and understood from the highway. The owner of any such sign, and the occupier of any land or premises where it is placed, are obliged under the terms of the Order to remove it at once, and if they do not do so the police are empowered to act in default.   As regards small notices of such a character that the place-name cannot easily be read from the highway, Chief Officers of Police have discretion to give an exemption to such extent and subject to such conditions as they may think fit.   Failure to comply with the terms of the Order is an offence under the Defence Regulations.

June 28/40   Dorking Council.   Mr. Hatswell wanted a bigger supply of steel helmets.   There were at Westcott, he said, 25 to 50 wardens who had among them only 10 helmets.   Mr. Somner:"We are trying to get more helmets.   The wardens are not expected to be out in the streets during an actual raid. The L.D.V. are, and when I tell you that there are Local Defence Volunteers without a helmet between them, you will realise that there is a difficulty".

July 5/40   Sandbag Filling.   Volunteers are urgently needed to help the Dorking L.D.V. by filling sandbags.   Men ready to help should go either to the sandpit in Vincent Lane or to the sand digging pit on the Dorking by-pass road any evening from 7.30 onwards, on Saturday afternoon from 2 p.m.,and at any time on Sunday from 9 a.m. There is a week's work to be done, and the Urban District Council are anxious that the work shall be done within the next week.   Men offering to do sandbag filling should, if possible, bring their own shovels.   Sandbag filling is good healthy exercise.

August 13/1976   When Vaughan Williams filled sandbags. A wartime memory of the late Dr. Ralph Vaughan Williams comes from Mrs. Gwen Gordon Clark of Wyatt House, Mickleham, who was reminded of it with the recent performance of his Symphony No. 6 at the Proms.

The music transported her back to 1939-40 when her late husband, Michael Gordon Clark, was in his third year as chairman of Dorking Council and second-in-command of the L.D.V. By August 1940 it was known as the Home Guard.

A German invasion was expected daily and an appeal went out for volunteers to fill sandbags at the vicarage sandpits.

South Holmwood Auxiliary Fire Service squad. *See page 24*

Dorking A.R.P. Ambulance Service, women ambulance drivers. *See page 26*

23

On the appointed day Mr. Gordon Clark was there early, ready to deal with the rush of eager workers. In fact there wasn't a rush. But among the few who answered the call was Dr. Vaughan Williams, shovel at the ready.

Mr. Gordon Clark was reluctant to see the great musician engaged on such a task. "What about your work?" he asked. The reply was "How can I do my work when my country is in danger?"

Symphony No. 6, says Mrs. Gordon Clark, expresses too, many of his feelings about the time in which they lived.

Mrs. Gordon Clark tells another story about the issue of Home Guard uniform at that time.

The local detachment had only one which would fit a man six feet or seven in height. And that meant that two lofty brothers at Westcott, Donovan and George Touche, could never be on duty together as they had to share it!

July 12/40 The Holmwood A.F.S. Squad has been provided with a trailer pump, and they are now anxious to secure a car in order that they may use their pump. It is thought there may be a resident in the village who has a car of something over 12-h.p. which he or she is not using at the present time, and who might be glad for it to be used on work of national importance.

July 12/40 The recently opened Toc H Services Club at Dorking is already doing splendid work and filling a real need. With the valuable assistance of a number of voluntary women workers, over 1000 light meals are being served each week and the club has a well equipped games room, including a full size billiard table and a reading and writing room. The club is open each evening from 6.30 to 10.30, and on Saturday and Sunday from 2.30.

July 19/40 All civilian respirators are to be fitted with a new filter to make them impervious to a gas against which they are not, as originally issued, entirely proof.

July 19/40 L.D.V. Parade - Dorking Local Defence Volunteers had their first ceremonial parade last Sunday afternoon. It was an impressive affair. The men on the march, headed by a drum and fife band from the Reigate Grammar School, made a stirring sight. They marched excellently. Beribboned veterans of the last war, with a considerable sprinkling of younger men, marched smartly, maintaining perfect alignment and showing the alertness of men ready to meet any emergency. The Volunteers, all in uniform, marched from the Drill Hall to the Nower, where photographs were taken. Then they marched via Coldharbour Lane into Horsham Road, where Major G.E.W. Lane, officer commanding the battalion, took the salute. They marched on to the Drill Hall, where they were addressed by Major Lane. He complimented them upon their smart appearance, and spoke to them of the importance of the work they were doing.

One of the three small craters at Sondes Place farm.   *See page 32*

Lady Reading, National Chairman of the W.V.S. on her visit to Dorking.   *See page 26*

July 19/40 Dorking A.R.P. Ambulance Service. A group of women ambulance drivers and drivers of cars for sitting cases. With the exception of four, these drivers are voluntary, unpaid workers. They are trained and ready for any emergency.

July 26/40 Lady Reading, National Chairman of the Women's Voluntary Services of which she was the founder, visited Dorking on Wednesday morning.

Before going on to the next town in her programme of visits - Guildford - Lady Reading went to the nursery school established by the Dorking W.V.S. for the benefit of young evacuated children at the Christian Alliance Women and Girls Hall in Junction Road. This was the first nursery school for evacuated children to be opened in this country. Lady Reading was much interested in the working of the school.

July 26/40 The name "Dorking" has been defaced temporarily from all conspicuous places along our streets, and from most of the vans operating in the town and district. There remain, however, the glaring exceptions of vehicles belonging to the D.U.D.C. These still carry the word "Dorking". Several people have written and spoken to us complaining that the local Council, who should show an example, do not do what the ordinary citizens have done to hide the name of the district. We understand that there is a good reason for this. The Council vehicles have to be prepared to do convoy work in a big area extending over six counties. To avoid confusion at the point of assembly, the convoy vehicles have to bear the name of their town of origin. In an emergency, the names could be quickly covered or removed.

July 26/40 On Sunday last in the Dorking Urban District, the air raid wardens, aided by Boy Scouts, fitted 15000 new filters to civilian respirators. The total of respirators in the possession of local residents is 23400, so there are many still not fitted with the new filter. Those residents whose respirators have not been attended to, should take their respirators to the nearest wardens' post as soon as possible, and in any case not later than July 31st. The wardens' posts, excepting those at North Holmwood and Mickleham, are open all day and night.

August 2/40 Dorking Council. The Chairman reported that Dr. Vaughan Williams had given free of charge the use of land forming part of his kitchen garden for four war-time allotment plots.

The Survey reported that the concrete shelters for the public had been completed at a cost of £714, the original contract price being £737.

The A.R.P. Officer was authorised to buy berets at 11d. each for male A.R.P. personnel already supplied with uniforms.

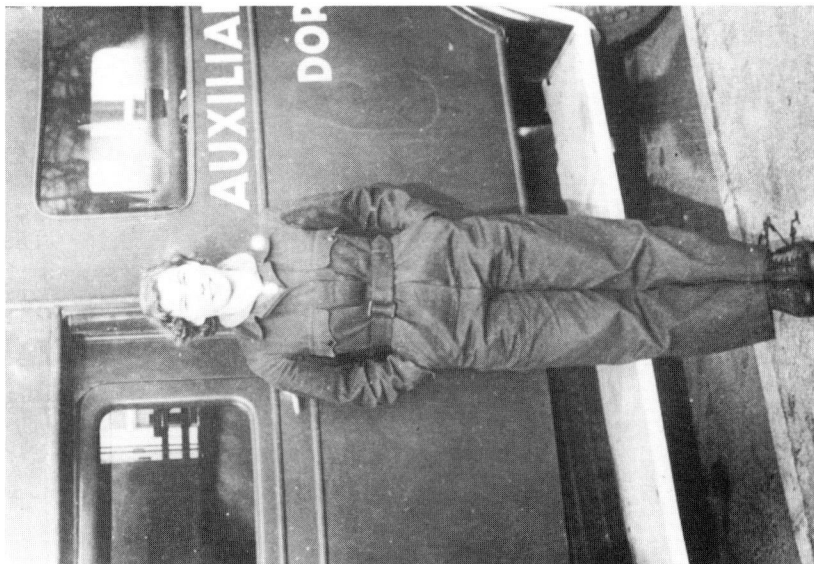

Miss Honorine Williamson — In the Dorking A.R.P. Service.
See page 36

Miss Kathleen Spooner — Fire watcher from Hart Road.
See page 28

August 2/40 Ockley man wounded. A Home Guard sentry fired at a car which, it is alleged, failed to stop after it had been challenged by a road patrol in Stane street, Ockley, on Wednesday evening. A passenger in the car Robert Munro who is employed as a chauffeur by Mr. R.D. Trotter of Leith Vale, Ockley, was seriously wounded.

It is understood Munro was sitting in the back of the car, in which there were four passengers in addition to the driver. The shot narrowly missed another occupant, going over his shoulder, tearing his coat and hitting Munro in the back. He was attended by Dr. Ward Clark and taken to Dorking Hospital. His condition, after a blood transfusion, is stated to be serious.

August 2/40 By neighbourly co-operation, emergency fire parties are being formed in several Dorking streets and are being prepared to cope with incendiary bombs and small fires occurring during possible air raids. In Marlborough Road, Beresford Road and Lyons Court, Fireman Cullum, assisted by air raid wardens, has collected £8 with which to buy six stirrup pumps. The pumps are now on order and are expected to be available within a few days. Two pumps will be allocated to each of the streets named and in each street there will be two squads of five men ready for action if necessity arises. Members of the squads are receiving instructions at the Fire Station in the use of stirrup pumps - similarly in Hart Road and Hart Gardens, the wardens have arranged for eight stirrup pumps to be bought and kept in readiness for emergencies, with trained parties to operate each pump. Residents of the streets are sharing the cost of the pumps. Delivery of the pumps is expected shortly.

August 16/40 The Toc H Club for Servicemen, which was opened at premises in High Street some weeks ago, appears to be developing into something bigger than the local officers of Toc H had anticipated. Between 2000 and 3000 meals are being served each week, and about 10 cwt. of potatoes are being consumed weekly.

August 16/40 One hundred and twenty stirrup pumps bought by the Dorking W.V.S. have arrived and are now being distributed among the people who ordered them a few weeks ago. The story of the buying of these pumps makes another instance of the readiness and efficiency with which the W.V.S. can do public service, but the story is not so creditable to the Dorking Urban District Council. In June, the Surrey Regional Controller for A.R.P. wrote to all local authorities in his area drawing attention to the Government's wish that stirrup pumps should be made available to the public who want to buy pumps to deal with incendiary bomb fires. The Regional Controller suggested to the local authorities two ways in which pumps could be obtained - either the Council could buy the pumps direct from the manufacturers for resale to the public or they could order through local ironmongers. Of course, the larger the number of pumps ordered the lower the price. The pump manufacturers required pre-payment - 25% with the order and the balance upon the pumps being ready

28

for delivery. The Dorking Council, almost alone among Surrey local authorities, declined to take any steps towards buying pumps. They contended that Councils are not allowed to engage in trade, although in fact the trading they were asked to do would not have been profit making trade, for the exact amount of money expended would have been recovered from the householders who had ordered the pumps. The Council also objected to advancing money to pay for goods before delivery. In their letter declining to order the pumps, the Council referred to "the great difficulty experienced in obtaining pumps for the Council's own services."

In the meantime, many Dorking householders were anxiously trying to buy stirrup pumps so as to form private emergency fire parties, generally with a pump to each four or five houses and with the neighbours of these houses co-operating together in meeting the cost of the pump and in organising themselves into a crew for operating the pump when necessary. So the W.V.S. stepped in and promptly climbed over the brick wall against which the Urban Council stood adamant. W.V.S. members took orders from shopkeepers and householders requiring pumps and sent to the manufacturers an order for 120 pumps. Many more than 120 orders could have been secured but, as there had to be pre-payment to the manufacturers, the W.V.S. thought that advancing cash for 120 pumps was the limit to which they could go. The money was advanced privately by W.V.S. members and within four weeks the 120 pumps have been delivered. They are now being distributed among the people who had ordered them and the price of 20s.6d. per pump is being collected to repay the money advanced. The Dorking and Horley Rural District Council, not being as timid as the Urban Council, ordered 400 pumps to resell to the public and have had delivery.

August 23/40 Westcott. Jam making and bottling - acting in conjunction with the Westcott Grow More Food Committee, the Womens Institute in the village have bottled or made into jam over two and a half hundredweight of plums. This produce is being sold at not less than market prices from a small shop, kindly lent to the Committee, situated in Westcott Street.

August 30/40 Growing Food at Westcott. Sir:- Because it is estimated that about 1000 people in the village read your paper weekly, the Grow More Food Committee of Westcott would be grateful if you would publish the following remarks and aims arising from their first meeting.

The aim is that Westcott will not only be self supporting in fresh vegetables and root crops but also be able to supply part of Dorking. With this end in view, the Committee wish to divide the area into wards, each of which should be in charge of a professional gardener or others who would be ready to give expert advice and be helpful in every way - volunteers are needed for this work. A centre has been lent for the grading and packing of supplies for the wholesale trade. The monies received will be paid to the growers. One village has already promised to send its surplus to Westcott to help make up the quantities demanded by the trade for each consignment. Smaller quantities will be sold at the shop at not less than market prices but the Committee intend to deal and work as much as possible with the local traders.

There will be no difficulty in obtaining allotments for those who need them, and it is hoped that in view of the urgency, those already possessing land will dig up new plots. The Women's Institute have set a splendid example by not only bottling and jamming over three hundredweight of plums (now being sold at the shop) but also by clearing, digging and sowing a plot of land they have acquired.

The Committee hope that all who can will get down to the job of digging for victory, and they in their turn will do all in their power to help, encourage, advise, and if necessary will purchase seeds and fertilisers at cheaper rates for distribution at cost price. There should be little or no trouble about a market. The problem at the present moment is to increase production so that our brothers and sisters in the towns will not go short. Indeed, increasing production is one way of fulfilling the law of loving your neighbour, so please "Go to it". - Yours etc., F.E. Hatswell. Chairman. F.W.G. Clinton. Hon. Secretary. Westcott.

August 30/40 Strange how the Dorking Urban District Council resent even the slightest suggestion of criticism. Dorking's slogan should be "Pippbrook is always right". A fortnight ago, we told the story of how a private organisation, W.V.S., obtained a supply of stirrup pumps after the Council has declined to order a supply, although they had been asked to do so by the Council A.R.P. Controller. The story was told plainly and accurately. It did not, by the way, come from the W.V.S. The only suggestion of criticism we made against the Council was that they had been timid. We knew that their reason for not ordering stirrup pumps was a fear of indulging in municipal trading and we said so. In any case, whether criticism of the Council was justified may be judged from the fact that, while the Council dallied with the idea of ordering pumps, private enterprise stepped in, ordered the pumps, got the supply, and sold them to the public who were clamouring for them. The result proves that the criticism was justified. We repeat that the Council were timid although their reasons for being timid may have appeared to them to have been sound.

August 30/40 Hurricane P3203 of 79 Squadron from Biggin Hill - collided with a Heinkel He 111 of 10/K.G.1 during combat over Reigate at 11.10 am. Crashed near Swires Farm near Henfold Lane. P/O Morris baled out unhurt, landing near Dorking.

September 6/40 Heinkel destroyed after dropping bombs on Surrey town. Bombs were dropped on the outskirts of a Surrey town (Dorking) during the enemy's big scale raid over South-East England last Friday morning. There were a few casualties. One man - not a resident of the district - who was riding a motor cycle when a bomb fell near him was severely injured, partly by the force of the bomb explosion and partly by falling from the motor cycle. He died early the following day. A man, aged 85, died suddenly through hurrying home after the air raid warning sounded. He was a resident of the Almshouses and when the air raid started he was walking back to the Almshouses after drawing the old age pension at the Post Office. His death was afterwards certified to be due to natural causes.

Those were the fatal casualties. The other casualties were for the most part not serious.

The damage done, too, was not serious. Excepting for a bomb crater in a road, (Westcott Road) temporarily stopping traffic and breaking the gas main, none of the damage could be said to have any military significance.

Very quickly after the bombs dropped in the outskirts of the town, the enemy paid the penalty. One of his bombers, shot down by a Spitfire, crashed on farmland between four and five miles from the town.

At about the same time as the bombs were falling, the sound of machine gun firing was heard from a high altitude, and bullets fell in various parts of the town. In the fighting, a Spitfire was attacking Messerschmitts which were escorting a Heinkel bomber. The Spitfire accidently collided with the Heinkel. The Spitfire pilot baled out and descended safely. (The pilot's name was Pilot Officer E.J. Morris a South African of 79 Squadron and the plane was a Hurricane not a Spitfire. The German plane was a Heinkel III.) The Heinkel crashed near a farm and three of its crew were killed instantly in the crash (The farm was Swires Farm in Henfold Lane on the way to Newdigate.) The captain of the Heinkel took to his parachute. He had, however, severe head injuries, there is a chance that he may lose his eyesight.

When the Heinkel crashed, a squad of soldiers rushed across a field to it in a lorry. Just as they reached the Heinkel, its load of bombs exploded. The soldiers scattered, luckily without receiving any injury. Through the explosion of the bombs, the wreckage of the Heinkel was set alight and the fire spread to the Army lorry and to some trees. Also the explosion severely damaged the interior of the neighbouring farmhouse and of another house, and broke windows in other houses in the vicinity. Detachments of three fire brigades, including A.F.S. men attended to deal with the fires caused by this explosion.

The Hurricane which had collided with the Heinkel crashed in a field a few hundred yards away from its victim, doing no material damage.

Doctor injured. Of the bombs that fell in the outskirts of the town, the one that caused most of the casualties made a big crater in a road. (Westcott Road). A fragment of this bomb injured a local doctor, (Dr. Billings of Westcott) who was motoring to his A.R.P. post. The bomb fragment struck him on the head. On a seat in his car, he had his "tin hat". Had he been wearing it, his injuries would probably not have been as serious as they were.

That bomb crater was 18 feet across and 7 feet deep. There were three smaller craters nearby. One bomb fell on a country mansion (Sondes Place) and another fell so close to a house as to damage it considerably (Milton Court). But there were no serious casualties through those bombs, and one bomb at least seemed to be an oil incendiary bomb. It made a deep hole in the ground at the edge of a wood, burning in the hole for a long time and setting fire to adjoining undergrowth.

One elderly man who was standing in a street was slightly injured by a spent machine gun bullet which struck him on the shoulder. There were five craters in a line across fields in which cattle were grazing. Two heifers were injured and had to be destroyed. Some small pigs were burnt alive through an incendiary bomb falling in their pen.

The following account about this incident was published in "The Henley Telegraph" Milton Court, Dorking. Vol.VIII. Autumn 1940- No.61.

"A Bit of Blitz. The skies spewed death."

"As near as we can remember that is the note we made in our diary on Saturday, August 31st, to record the happenings of the previous day. August 30th was a brilliant day which, so the experts have told us since, came at the end of the driest August since 1818. Skies were blue, the air was delightful and for our part we were walking along one of the corridors with an army officer when the first bell rang "air raid warning". Within three minutes after showing the army officer with a carefree wave of the hand where the baronial kitchens used to be, we arrived at the front entrance just at the moment the warning bells clanged. We stayed to collect our gas masks and a few chocolates, waved airily to the army officer as he walked across to his motor bike to chug off down the drive, strolled the first few yards on our way to the shelters, casually noted a "zooming" almost above our heads, and then heard the first "crump". And so we bit the gravel, raised our head for a split moment to decide whether we could take the flight of six stone steps in one bound, heard the crash of more bombs and the whistle of flying shard from the bursts and decided we couldn't, and then noted the staccato rattle of machine guns just above our head. So we tucked ourselves as far as we could into the comforting protection of an ivy covered balustrade and an overhanging wistaria, and "waited for it".

August 30th was as someone has already called it - Miracle Day. A Board Meeting was in progress not more than 50 yards - if that - from where two of the bombs burst, and in a direct line with them. Many of the staff were in the open and on their way to the trenches when the splinters were flying; and the only two casualties - Howell and Ringer, car drivers - although merely a few yards from two of the bursting bombs escaped with what were in the circumstances slight wounds. One house had its roof smashed, and suffered some other minor damage; some of the windows of another were broken; when things had quietened down, ugly looking splinters were picked up from spots where people on their way to the trenches had passed during the bombing; and several cars were damaged.

The staff behaved admirably, biting the dust like veterans, and for the A.R.P. service generally - men and women, too - there was nothing but praise. Some of the firemen in the fire station near the lakeside had escapes quite narrow enough to be distinctly memorable, splinters of bomb piercing the structure while the firemen were adopting the orthodox prone position.

The bombs on the estate were not the only ones that morning. Many more fell not far away. British fighters chased the Nazi bombers who, we calculate, disposed of their loads in order to attempt a get away. So ended the incident, for in a war such as this, that is all it was".

September 13/40   A Dorking Fire crew's experiences at London Docks blaze. A crew of Dorking firemen with a heavy trailer pump drawn by a Rolls Royce car converted into a fire tender, joined the hundreds of fire crews and appliances which fought the fires in the London Docks area after Saturday evening's raid.

"When I left home on Saturday evening to report at the Dorking Fire Station for duty", (writes our Dorking representative, Mr. A.G. Williams, who is a sub-officer of the Dorking Auxiliary Fire Service), "I saw the huge glow in the sky over Box Hill". "They will be wanting you tonight, Dad - good luck", was the parting greeting from one of my sons. That glow certainly looked like a big job for firemen but I did not expect to be among the thousands of firemen there.

A telephone call came to the Dorking Fire Station asking for a pump and crew to be sent to a Thames side Middlesex town, well West of London. The Dorking Chief Officer ordered me to go in charge of the "Apex" crew. ("Apex" is the manufacturer's name of our heavy trailer pump). So away we went through the darkness, wondering what lay ahead. The sky was bright with searchlights but, under the trees along the country roads we were passing along for a great part of the way, it was exceedingly dark. And we did not know the way and our lights were dimmed. We were stopped a few times by military and Home Guards and we had to stop twice and ask the way. Then we came across a kindly motorist who was going our way. We followed his dim tail lamp for miles.

So we reached the Fire Station to which we were to report. Then, within a few minutes, guided by a fireman cyclist, we were moved to a big garage where dozens of fire crews and pumps were assembling. Here we enjoyed the warmth of a cup of tea, very

welcome after the long, anxious night ride, and we ate some of
the biscuits in the iron rations we were carrying on our tender.

After about three quarters of an hour of waiting while more
pump crews were assembling we were ordered to take a specified
position in a convoy of fire appliances which were to go to a
fire station in the north of London. Out we went again into the
night. The glow of the great London fires was on our right and
all around were the bursts of anti-aircraft fire. Occasionally
we heard the thud of bombs. But we did not have much chance nor
desire to look in any direction excepting that in which we were
going. The journey alone was sufficiently exciting. The fire
engines - 30 or 40 of them were in our convoy by this time - were
racing along at what seemed to be a terrific speed. At
roundabouts and corners, the speed dropped suddenly, brakes went
hard on and we, insignificant human beings on a hurtling fire
engine hung on, fearing each time that we would bump into the
pump in front or that the pump behind would crash into us.

However, we raced on safely, thanks to our magnificent driver,
a Dorking Motor Company mechanic. It was about 2 a.m. on Sunday
morning when our convoy arrived at the North London Fire Station.
Within a few minutes, new orders came. We were to go, this time
in a small convoy of 10 pumps, to a certain street in the East
End of London.

Going into the fire glow. On we went again, this time moving
directly towards the fire area, the glow of which we had first
seen from Dorking. Soon the fires gave us enough light to make
our own driving lights unnecessary. Although our speed continued
to be quite thrilling enough for our peace of mind, other fire
engines passed us travelling even faster, all moving towards the
fire area. At the sides of the roads were empty buses and other
vehicles, abandoned when the air raid began. Practically the
only traffic on the road were the fire appliances.

We were getting close to the fires now, going under the pall of
smoke clouds, feeling the heat. We did not mind the heat then
because we who were sitting outside on the fire tender were cold.
We could see great blazes where buildings were alight and sparks
were dancing up into the smoke clouds.

Then we reached our ordered destination- a street in which six
tall buildings were blazing fiercely, all within a hundred yards
or so, with other fires from the docks area in the near distance.
Here we stopped for a quarter of an hour. There were hundreds of
firemen hard at work with great mazes of delivery hose running
over the roads and pavements. Immediately to our right, there
was a fire tower from the top of which a fireman was directing a
jet of water into a blazing building.

Again new orders came. We were to turn round and hurry to one
of the great London docks. So, bumping over the delivery hose
where it lay across the roads, we went to dockland. We passed
the Monument - the memorial to that other great London fire - and

we passed over London Bridge. The streets we passed through were deserted. Enemy raiders were still overhead and the occupants of the houses must have been in the air raid shelters. Anti-aircraft guns were still sending up occasional bursts. The searchlight beams were almost lost in the glow of the fires.

We passed demolished buildings, gaunt ghosts of a horrible night. Once we nearly came to grief. The nearside wheels of our tender were within an inch of the edge of a bomb crater. At last we turned into the docks entrance. Two hundred yards ahead was a blazing ship and an inferno of flames. We pulled into the side of the road, dismounted and immediately had to take cover by the side of a wall as bombs fell. An hour passed. We could see crowds of firemen ahead of us while we awaited orders to be called into action.

Then happily, the "All Clear" sounded and we were able to get away from the protecting wall. Soon after that we got to work. We were ordered to take our pump alongside one of the dock basins and pump water on to stacks of blazing timber to prevent the flames from spreading. In this work we joined other pumps from various parts of London and the Home Counties. We sent jets of water under high pressure onto the blazing timber for nearly six hours. It was tiring work, holding the branches, and hot and thirsty work too. We had to move quickly sometimes because around us were the pillars of what had been open timber sheds. The roofs had been burnt through and had fallen, but many of the pillars and iron girders remained and we had to take care that they did not collapse on us.

There was a movable hoisting crane at the spot where we were working and the craneman's hut supported on pillars 25 feet high was still smouldering. Occasionally it would burst into flames again and we had to direct a jet of water on to it. We stood ankle deep in a mixture of charred timber, ashes and water.

Two hundred yards to our right there were two burnt out trailer pumps standing amid heaps of ashes - grim reminders of what our colleagues of the London Fire Brigade had endured when, as we had been told earlier that morning they had to abandon some of their appliances and run for their lives because enemy raiders returned to drop more bombs and start new fires.

We worked on until one by one the pumps gave out as their petrol tanks emptied. Of the pumps in this particular part of the fire area, the Dorking pump was the last to stop work. It had run perfectly smoothly, registering a steady 100 lbs. pressure, for nearly six hours.

While London Fire Brigade officers were sending for more petrol, we rested and ate more of our iron rations. Then the air raid warnings sounded. By this time some of the pumps had restarted work with fresh supplies of petrol. As the sirens sounded, the London Fire Brigade officer in charge ordered "Stop pumping", and all the firemen hurried into the air raid shelters.

35

As we sat in the shelter, weary through hard work and lack of sleep, we were surprised to hear a call: "Is a Dorking crew here?" Out I went to find that a relief crew of A.F.S. men had been sent from the Dorking Fire Station. Soon after that, we were in the fire tender (a converted private car) in which the relief crew had come and we returned to Dorking, leaving our colleagues to carry on.

The next day, we learnt that the relief crew had worked at fighting the timber fire for over seven hours throughout Sunday afternoon and evening. By blackout time that evening,the fires were, for the most part, smouldering heaps. The relief crew were dismissed then but just as they had "made up" (that is, collected their delivery, branches etc.) the air raid warnings sounded and they had to dive to shelter. They stayed in the shelter all night while bombs again fell around the docks area, starting some new fires. The Dorking firemen came through safely and, in the early morning returned home.

While the relief crew were in the shelter, we of the first "Apex" crew were sleeping soundly at our homes and, in the morning, we returned to our normal civilian occupations, still a bit tired, perhaps, but feeling that we had had an experience that we would not have missed for worlds - an unforgettable night and day".

September 13/40   Three high explosive bombs were dropped on a village on Saturday evening causing minor casualties and damage to residential property. It is believed the bombs were released after the enemy plane had been caught in the beam of a searchlight.

One bomb dropped between two houses, and the owner of one of these houses, Mr. T.R. McMillan, (Deerleap Cottage, Deerleap Road, Westcott), who was apparently standing under the loggia, was injured by shrapnel, which hit him in the leg and shoulder. His house was considerably damaged.

Other casualties included a maid, who was having a bath and was slightly injured when the ceiling fell in, and another girl. In one house an evacuee boy slept soundly through it all. Shrapnel went through the bedroom window and made a hole in the ceiling, but it was not until after he had been awakened and told, that he knew what had happened.

In the same village damage was done to some cottages, one or two being temporarily uninhabitable.

September 20/40   The funeral took place at Dorking Cemetery on Wednesday of Mrs. Honorine Brown. She was Miss Honorine Williamson, a niece of Dr. R.O. Morris, professor at the Royal College of Music and brother-in-law of Dr. Vaugham Williams. She was part of the Vaugham Williams household for about twelve years just before the war.

Honorine married Bernard Brown the trumpeter. Bernard served in the Irish Guards and was based in London during the Blitz. On the night of September 2nd 1940, he and Honorine were bombed in their London house and trapped in the wreckage. He was saved but she was killed.

September 27/40 Westcott's First Aid Point (Dorking Council). The A.R.P. Committee reported the receipt of a letter signed by several of the volunteers manning the unofficial first aid point at Westcott. The Committee resolved that efforts be made to assure Westcott residents that the district was fully protected by the Council's existing casualty services; and that a meeting be arranged with a few influential residents of Westcott with a view to the organisation of a first aid point.

Mr. Hatswell hoped the meeting would be arranged as soon as possible. He was certain it was the Council's duty to ensure that first aid points were established in the villages and made efficient and staffed at the earliest possible moment.

September 27/40 Last week, Mr. J.F. Somner (Vice Chairman of the D.U.D.C.) who is an officer of the Home Guard, went into a South Eastern county with a military lorry and some soldiers to get bedding for refugees. The party came to a place where an enemy aircraft's bombs exploded. Pieces flew in all directions. Fortunately without seriously injuring anyone. The force of the explosions threw Mr. Somner to the ground. He was hurt slightly and the terrific noise and blast of the explosions caused temporary deafness.

October 4/40 Two houses demolished. Five killed in South-East village. A number of bombs fell in a village (Brockham, Nutwood Avenue) during Friday night, and one demolished two adjoining houses, causing casualties, five of them fatal. In one house, Mrs. Daisy Herrington, her five year old daughter June, and George Alan Wilfred Biggs an evacuee, were killed, and in the next house, Mrs. Esther Eva Fisher and William John, her younger son aged 2, were killed. Mrs. Fisher's elder boy, aged four and a half, and her sister, were injured. Mrs. Herrington's husband is in the R.A.F, and Mr. Fisher was away from home at the time on A.F.S duty. The other bombs caused no damage. A rescue party worked heroically throughout the night to get the victims out of the debris.

At about the same time incendiary bombs were dropped on an adjoining parish, but there no casualties, and no damage was caused.

Three high explosive bombs fell close together near the centre of a town on Saturday night (Rose Hill, Dorking) but surprisingly, did very little damage and there were no casualties. One landed within a few yards of a surface air raid shelter, among the occupants of which were three children, who were not even awakened by the noise. All the damage this bomb did, apart from making a big crater in the side of the road, was to wreck a wooden shed and demolish part of two walls. A second bomb fell on the lawn at the back of a doctor's house, (Dr. McComas) and the third close to the front of another big house. A number of broken windows was the extent of the damage done by all three bombs to shops and private houses. Many incendiary bombs fell on houses and in open country in the South West of the town, but again the damage was very slight. The majority of the fires which resulted were put out by the occupants of houses with stirrup pumps, which more than proved their value, but in a number of cases fire brigade crews had to be called to deal with outbreaks. During the night, many high explosive and incendiary bombs were dropped in open country to the West and South of the town. On the Eastern outskirts of the same town, four high explosives fell harmlessly in a field.

Nazi descends on Dorking. Hundreds of people and scores of cars and motor cycles raced to the scene when the pilot of a German fighter, which crashed at Kingswood, descended by parachute in Yew Tree Road, Dorking on Monday. Badly burnt about the face and head, the pilot was unconscious when he landed and was rushed to hospital.

On Friday morning people in the Dorking district had a grandstand view of an aerial engagement which was the prelude to a highly successful day for our Fighter Command and anti-aircraft defences. As a formation of enemy planes approached, violent anti-aircraft fire was heard and the last of the raiders - A Junkers 88 - was hit. This was one of the first of a bag of 133 brought down during the day. (In "Battle over Britain" by Francis K. Mason, 1969 it states that 65 German planes were lost that day in the entire Luftwaffe.) As the machine began to fall, in flames and out of control, four airmen were seen to bale out - some say there was a fifth, but there appears to have been no news of his having landed in the immediate district. One of the airmen came down at Bradley Farm, about a mile out of the town, another at Scammells Farm, Blackbrook, and a third near the Norfolk Arms, Mid-Holmwood. Two of these were slightly injured and all three were captured and taken by the military. The fourth airman when he reached the ground, in the Leatherhead district, without his parachute, was dead (he was Unteroffizier Menningmann.)

The plane, after setting fire to a haystack in its descent, buried itself in the ground at Folly Farm, South Holmwood. The rear gun turret and gun fell in the garden of Mr. E.S. Jones, at Folkington, Pilgrims Close, Westhumble. It was carried away by the police and military. Sightseers crowded to see the souvenir and £2 was collected from them for the Red Cross. Part of the tail came down in Croft Avenue, Dorking. This was exhibited in the saloon bar of a nearby hotel and during the day over £3 was

One of the German parachutists who landed at Bradley farm.
See page 42

The army with the captured German's parachute. *See page 42*

39

Rose Hill bomb crater and the wrecked wooden shed. See page 38

The engine of the Nazi bomber on display at the Dorking Halls 1977. See page 42

Rose Hill bomb damage — the crater and Butter Hill House.   *See page 38*

Rose Hill bomb crater and fallen telegraph pole.   *See page 38*

41

collected for the Dorking District Spitfire Fund. No bombs were dropped during the engagement.

October 4/40   On Friday of last week the German airman (Menningmann) fell in the sewage beds of an urban district (Leatherhead) in the South-Eastern area, when his parachute failed to open. He was buried in the parish churchyard on Thursday, and a short committal service was conducted by the Vicar of the parish. Only the undertakers and the verger were present at the service.

In 1976 the Surrey and Sussex Aviation Society carried out a dig at Folly Farm - they found oxygen bottles, a buckled Luger pistol 7.92 calibre, magazines with twisted ammunition inside, maps and note books, and a decayed life raft.

An engine was found at a depth of 26 feet and a propeller hub. The second engine was found about 15 feet from the first.

This German bomber was intercepted on the morning of 27th September 1940, at 9.00 a.m. over Oxted. A chase by a Hurricane which caused the bomber to catch fire near Esher. The plane flew on until it reached Leatherhead where the crew baled out, three became prisoners of war and the fourth member fell out of his parachute harness when the buckle became released. He crashed to earth, while his parachute sailed onto land in the grounds of Holmwood Park.

Apart from Unteroffizier Menningmann who was killed, the crew were Unteroffiziers Ackerman, Tenholt and Schumann. Their home base was near Amiens in France. Two out of the three survivors are still alive today (1977) in West Germany.

A year later the engine of this Nazi bomber shot down in 1940 took one more flight - across the Atlantic to Canada. It was destined for the Ottawa National War Museum as a gift from the Surrey and Sussex Aviation Society.

The plane enthusiasts dug the engine from the buried wreckage of a Junkers Ju. 88 which crashed at Folly Farm, Holmwood.

Before it was crated for its last flight, it went on display at Dorking Halls along with an array of other flight relics uncovered through the years. Along for the show were some of Air Canada's top brass, including Canadian High Commission senior liaison officer.

October 4/40   The editor of the Dorking Advertiser writes, "I am asked to pass on a suggestion from the A.R.P. authorities of a certain district which might well apply to all areas. It is that people who spend the nights, or part of them, in air raid shelters away from their homes, should pin on the door of their residence notification of the fact and where they can be found if required. This would save the A.R.P. authorities a lot of time in the event of emergencies arising".

October 18/40   Took part of Nazi plane.   Reigate man summoned at Dorking.   Stated to have taken part of a crashed German aeroplane on August 30th in order that it might be placed in a window at Reigate where parts of enemy planes were exhibited in aid of the Spitfire Fund.   A.B., a member of the Home Guard, of West Street Reigate, pleaded guilty at Dorking Police Court on Wednesday to removing part of the magneto from a crashed German plane.

Attempts to remove parts of plane.   A soldier, Sergt. Ewell said he was assisting the police and the military in forming a cordon round the wrecked plane - a German bomber which had crashed and blown up.   He saw A.B. walking away with what appeared to be a very bulky package in his blouse.   A.B. told witness he was going to dump it, he would not have had it in his blouse.   A.B. was in uniform and, witness thought, he had a rifle.   Witness took it for granted he was on duty and was assisting in guarding the wreckage.

Mr. Pringle (representing A.B.), addressing the magistrates said A.B. was not on guard.   He was a member of a platoon in another district and, having heard of this crash, was given an opportunity of a lift to go and see it.   While he was there, unfortunately misdirected zeal overcame him.   There was a window in Reigate where parts of German aeroplanes were exhibited in order to attract subscriptions to the Spitfire Fund.   In his ignorance, A.B. gathered that these had been collected in the way in which he meant to collect a part - by taking them and surreptitiously carry them away.   It was not a dereliction of duty, it was misdirected zeal.

The Chairman (Mr. W.A. Calvert) said this was the first case of the kind that had come before the Bench.   He thought A.B. must know, as most members of the public knew, that the regulation against people taking pieces of anything that came down in an enemy crash was made because any piece might lead to discoveries which might be of value.   It seemed essential that, when an aeroplane crashed, all the parts should be left alone.   A.B. was apparently trying to do something to help, but that should make him more particular in carrying out the regulations.   Under the circumstances, this being the first case of its kind, the Bench wished to give him a very serious caution against actions of this sort, and the case would be dismissed.

Most young boys during the war must have been suffering from misdirected zeal, judging by the amount of war souvenirs that were swopped at school.

October 18/40   Westcott and Shelters.
A well attended meeting was held in the Hut, Westcott, on Saturday, to discuss the question of the provision of air raid shelters in the village.

The Chairman, explaining the purpose of the meeting, reported

The first type of Air Raid Shelter at Ashley Road, Westcott. See page 45

Staff nurse Nan Jones in the uniform of Queen Alexandra's Imperial Military Nursing Service Reserve. P/O J. A. Milne the Canadian from 605 Squadron. See page 45

44

that over 400 signatures had been obtained for the petitions which were being sent to the Urban Council on this matter, while other sheets were still out for further signatures to be obtained.

The first speaker was Mrs. Hygate, who was responsible for the first part of the petition, and she expressed her dissatisfaction, which she thought was shared by everyone present, at the failure of the authorities to provide even a proper shelter for the children of the village.

Mr. F.E. Hatswell, the Urban Councillor for Westcott, spoke of the limitations placed upon local expenditure for air raid precautions by the Ministry of Home Security, and reported that a surface shelter, designed to hold 48 persons, was being erected in Ashley Road. There were also proposals, he said, for the strengthening of houses to withstand blast effects.

During the discussion which arose, many criticisms were made of the inadequacy of surface shelters, and speakers expressed the opinion that there was a need for those of the underground type. Suggestions were made on the possibility of digging into the surrounding hillsides to provide shelters.

In reply to the general dissatisfaction expressed, Mr. Hatswell proposed the following resolution, which was carried unanimously "At a meeting of Westcott ratepayers, held on Saturday, October 12th, it was resolved that adequate air raid shelters for the residents of Westcott should be provided in the village and at the school at the earliest possible moment".

October 22/40   Hurricane V6783 of 605 Squadron from Croydon, shot down at 2.30 p.m. over Dorking. P/O Milne a Canadian pilot, force landed on the railway bank near the old Westcott sewage works. He dislocated his hip.

P/O Milne states: "The Battle of Britain had cooled off some by the latter part of October. We were now looking for small groups or single bombers, mostly Ju 88's or high-flying Me 109's. A Me 109 dived down below us and pulled up under my tail. I remember the thumping and hurt on my back as the 20 mm. cannon shells penetrated my seat's armour plate and part of my parachute. I still have tiny bits in my back but fortunately the damage was not serious. However, he did smash part of the cockpit and certainly wrecked my engine which was emitting smoke back into the cockpit. I still had control of the aircraft and went into a spiral dive and dropped down about 12,000 feet. Now I was faced with the problem of to jump or not to jump. I feared my chute had been damaged which could make baling out rather dicey and at the same time my engine was smoking, which could present a risk of fire. I decided to ride it down and if fire broke out the decision was made for me, I would have to bale out. Afraid that during this time I had been losing altitude fast and landing areas around Dorking seemed pretty scarce, (fields were smaller in those days), I tried for a small open space not far from Dorking but on a dead stick final approach I failed to clear some trees.

I ended up in Dorking County Hospital and later transferred to Horton Hospital in Epsom.

While in Dorking Hospital I started dating Staff Nurse Nan Jones. We were married one year later".

October 25/40   The Superintendent of Police at Dorking appeals to the public to exercise more care in regard to their blackout arrangements. Many complaints have been received lately of lights showing from houses during darkness and in almost every case it is merely a question of carelessness rather than wilful neglect. Supt. Hilton points out that there have been instance in which it has been established that bombs have fallen in country districts because lights have been visible to enemy planes. Besides causing considerable uneasiness among their neighbours, people who do not take the trouble to see that their blackout is completely effective are placing themselves and others in danger. People are asked to go out and look round after they have put up their blackout just to make sure no light is escaping.

November 1/40   Nazi night raids. Bombs wreck houses. The Pavilion of a neighbouring village cricket club (Westcott) was destroyed when a bomb fell near it on Saturday night.

A large bomb fell near some allotment ground to the South of the town on Monday evening, but there was only slight damage to the roofs of some houses as the result of flying earth.

Two families bereaved. Some people were killed and two injured when a couple of high explosives wrecked two houses and did some damage to others on a housing estate in this town on Tuesday night (Fraser Gardens, Dorking). In one house, Mr. and Mrs. Evans were sitting round the fire, watching it burn out before they went to bed, when their house collapsed. They both escaped without injury. Their two daughters, one aged 20 and the other 12, who were upstairs, were killed but their two sons had fortunate escapes. One, aged 17, was blown out of bed by the blast, but was unhurt, and the other, aged 7, ran out of the wreckage into a neighbour's house. He was treated for a blow on the head, which was not very severe. Another fatal casualty was Mrs.Jordan, who lived next door. Her husband was injured. A lodger, Mr. Ede was also hurt and spent the night in the first aid post.

An oil bomb which fell in the front garden of a house on an adjoining estate made a nasty mess, but failed to ignite and caused no damage. This was at Parkway.

November 1/40   Dorking Council. The A.R.P. Committee considered a petition signed by Westcott residents applying for public shelters at Westcott. The Clerk said he had told the petitioners that the Council proposed to erect a public shelter at Westcott.

The Surveyor reported that the Regional Officer had approved the acceptance of Messrs. Trollope and Coll's tender for the construction of communal domestic shelters.

Dorking Firemen in London Fires.
The following letter came from the London Fire Brigade:- "I should like to express the appreciation of the London Regional Commissioners of the services of the crews of the 40 pumps which were sent from your Region to help us at an anxious period. Many of these crews came from long distances, and some of them included part-time personnel. They were employed at fires in Whitechapel and Shoreditch, where they cheerfully accepted bombing, inadequate food supplies, long hours and general discomfort. Comdr. Firebrace has told me how valuable was their ready and efficient help, and I hope you will find some means of conveying our thanks to them."

The Dorking Fire Brigade Committee receiving that letter, added their appreciation of the services rendered by the two crews from the Dorking Auxiliary Fire Service who assisted in extinguishing fires in London caused by enemy action.

November 8/40 To boost the local Spitfire Fund a German bomber is to be exhibited in Dorking from November 21st to December 3rd. It will be put in an enclosure in the Pippbrook grounds and the sum received through the small charge to be made to each person inspecting the enemy plane will be added to the District Spitfire Fund. The bomber coming to Dorking will be the one which, up to November 20th, has been exhibited at Sutton. Mr. Leslie J.V. Piper, Clerk to the Urban District Council is now making arrangements for the exhibition of the bomber at Pippbrook. A day and night guard will be necessary. It is hoped that members of the Home Guard and members of the Civil Defence Services will share the guard duties.

November 8/40 A valuable Spitfire Fund donation received at the "Dorking Advertiser" office this week was the sum of £6.6s. from the Pneumatic Tent Company Ltd., South Street, Dorking. This sum has been collected by charging 6d. per week per person to those members of the public who use the Company's air raid shelter at night.

November 8/40 The stringent necessity for the early morning blackout to be every bit as efficacious as that at night should hardly need stressing at this time of the year, yet, according to friends of mine who often come off Home Guard duty in the early hours of the morning, there are quite a number of householders locally who are not so careful in this matter as the interests of public safety demand. It is suggested that there are householders who seem to think that as daylight is only half an hour away strict adherence to the blackout is unnecessary. One friend was particularly aghast at two bad cases he came across in

Some of Dorking's aluminium scrap for the Spitfire Fund. *See page 47*

THE W.V.S. mobile canteen that went to Southampton on December 2nd. *See page 55*

the space of a week. One was the brilliantly illuminated window of a shop where the lights remained on for about a minute and a half - which is long enough for a bomb-aimer to get an idea of his target and the other was apparently the window of a house where a good wife was probably getting an early meal for a husband off to work, blissfully ignorant, perhaps, of the fact that the window was a radiant oblong amidst that peculiar blackness that precedes the dawn. In both cases, my friend states, the offenders were within a few yards of a railway station.

On November 9/40 Deepdene Station area and Dorking High Street were machine gunned by a German raider.
[From A.R.P. map of Dorking].

November 15/40   Westcott Deputation on Shelters.
A deputation of Westcott residents was received by the A.R.P. Committee of the D.U.D.C at its last meeting on the question of shelters in the village. The deputation expressed its dissatisfaction at the Council's continued failure to provide adequate shelters, despite the personal complaints, petitions and resolution that had already been sent them. Criticisms were also made of the type of shelter erected in one Dorking district as being inadequate and proposals were put forward that the area being particularly suitable for tunnelling, advantage should be taken of the natural features of the countryside to provide what would be really safe shelter. As one of the deputation pointed out, authorities owed it to the men in the Forces that their wives and children should be kept safely in their absence. In reply, the Chairman of the Committee welcomed the opinions set forth by the deputation and agreed that the small shelters already erected left much to be desired and that no more of this type was being built.(This is the first type, built in Ashley Road, Westcott. See photo). Furthermore, every consideration was being given to using the natural facilities of the area including tunnelling where suitable. The whole question of shelters in the district was being reviewed by the Council Surveyors, whose recommendations would be available in the near future. Questioned on the date when the already sanctioned shelter for Westcott would be commenced, the Chairman gave assurances that work would be started immediately.

November 15/40   The German bomber which is to be exhibited in Dorking on behalf of the local Spitfire Fund is so big and heavy that the original proposal to place it in the grounds of Pippbrook has had to be abandoned. Instead the bomber will be put on exhibition in an enclosure on Cotmandene. It will arrive in Dorking on Thursday next and will be on exhibition from the following day, November 22nd to December 3rd inclusive. A charge of 1s. will be made from 10 a.m. to 1 p.m. and a charge of 6d. from 1 p.m. to 5 p.m. with half prices to Servicemen and children. Probably arrangements will be made so that upon payment of an extra charge, people will be able to enter the bomber's cockpit. Bracelets made from the transparent material used for the windows of Spitfires, and brooches made in the form

49

of Spitfires will be on sale as mementoes of the occasion. The exhibition is being officially organised through the Urban District Council. Volunteers will act as attendants and guards, so that the expenses will be kept very low.

November 22/40 A.R.P. Controller summoned. Alleged blackout offence. It being alleged that an unscreened light showed from the premises occupied by the Surrey A.R.P. Control in High Street, Dorking, about half an hour after blackout on October 29th; the Controller was summoned at Dorking Police Court on Wednesday.

P.C. Blandford said that, at 6.35 p.m. he saw a very bright unscreened light showing from a window of the premises occupied by the Surrey Control. He knocked at the door several times and eventually someone from an upstairs window, asked what was the matter. He told that person a light was showing, and should be extinguished as quickly as possible. Witness waited and was joined by Inspector Collis, who ordered him to go in through the window and put the light out, because there was a crowd of people on the pavement, and they were adopting a rather hostile attitude. He entered the premises and extinguished the light. On November 5th he interviewed the Controller and told him he would be reported for the offence. He replied: "Right". The case was adjourned until the next Court for the Controller to attend. (I have found that most cases for this offence have been fined £1-£2).

November 22/40 A supply of ear plugs - to counteract the deafening effect of blast - is available for free issue to the public in the Dorking Urban District. People are asked to go to their nearest wardens post to collect the ear plugs required for members of their family.

November 22/40 The idea of exhibiting a German bomber on Cotmandene, Dorking, in aid of the local Spitfire Fund has been temporarily abandoned. The exhibition was to have begun today and continued until December 3rd. However, some people - more than was known at first - hold the view that the exhibition of a German bomber is likely to attract bombs from German raiders. Many of these objectors have this week put their objections into the form of a protest petition, and have sent it to the Dorking Council Offices where the bomber exhibition was being organised. As this petition is signed by 310 persons, and it has been backed up by other messages of protest sent to the Pippbrook offices and to the "Dorking Advertiser" office, the exhibition of the bomber has been deferred for the time being while the subject is being further investigated. It is felt that, apart from other considerations, it is not wise to stage an exhibition which is likely to cause further anxiety to people already harassed by war worries. In actual fact, several towns have had exhibitions of German bombers without being bombed during the exhibition, and the cases of the towns which have suffered from bombs during the exhibition of a German plane are merely coincidences. Nevertheless the Spitfire Fund organisers do not wish to do anything that might cause people to be more nervous nor to do anything that might jeopardise the success of the Fund. So the exhibition is being deferred and, possibly, abandoned altogether.

November 29/40 Although the exhibition of a German bomber to aid the Dorking Spitfire Fund has been deferred largely owing to a petition against the proposal being received by the U.D.C., it is upsetting to learn that a few, at least, of the signatures in the petition were not genuine. A resident in Deepdene Gardens has written indignantly to the Council protesting against his name and the names of his family being included in the petition without his knowledge and contrary to his opinions. In his letter, he alleges that a man called at his house while the maid was the only person there - the man said he wanted a list of the people living in the house in case the house was bombed. The maid gave the names which duly appeared in the petition although the persons concerned, far from objecting to the exhibition of a German bomber, wanted such an exhibition to take place. The Deepdene Gardens resident, in his letter, strongly objects to the cancellation of the exhibition for what he describes as "the faint-hearted and superstituous attitude" of a minority of the people.

November 29/40 Considerable ingenuity has been displayed in converting a barn at Westhumble into a cheery and comfortable canteen for members of the Services. The canteen is being voluntarily staffed by ladies living in the district, and men in the Services will be able to get refreshments and recreation. There will be occasional concerts for their entertainment. Mr. R.B. Bennett opened this canteen on Saturday, and Sir James Jeans came up from Somerset to be present at the ceremony.

December 6/40 The Controller at the Surrey A.R.P. Control Centre in Dorking High Street pleaded guilty at Dorking Police Court on Wednesday to allowing an unscreened light from his office to show during the blackout. He was fined £20.

December 6/40 Dorking Urban Council. Possibility of caves as air raid shelters.

The Surveyor reported to the A.R.P. Committee that he had inspected a considerable number of caves in Dorking. With one exception, he considered them to be unsuitable for adaption as public shelters. The exception was the cave at the rear of the premises of Messrs. B. Turner, Ltd, in the High Street. The Committee inspected the cave and then decided to ask for an inspection by the Regional Technical Adviser with a view to approval.

At a subsequent A.R.P. Committee meeting, the Surveyor presented plans for the adaptation of the cave at the rear of Messrs. Turner's premises at a cost of about £750. The cave would accommodate 420 persons, or, if three tier bunks were fitted, bunks for 200 persons and seating accommodation for about 100 persons.

The A.R.P. Committee recommended the Emergency Committee to authorise the Surveyor to proceed with the proposal, including the provision of bunks.

Miss Evans (Councillor) inquired whether any steps had been taken to find out whether the cave shelter would be utilised. At present it was a most eerie place and it was doubtful whether it would be much used.

The Chairman: "It will look very different when it is fitted up".

Mr. Somner said the Regional authorities had agreed that the cave had possibilities as a shelter. No claim was made that it was bombproof. In any case, the Council would have no power to go ahead with the scheme unless it was approved by the Regional Technical Advisors. The Council would not work on the lines of whether the shelter would be used or not. The appearance of the cave would be changed entirely when it had electric light, seating, roof supports and some flooring. He thought the shelter would be used.

The Surveyor recommended that basements at the following premises be again considered for use as shelters and that application be made to the Regional Officer for approval: Bembridge House, West Street; Milton Motors, High Street; and the Dorking Book Shop, South Street.

The Surveyor also recommended that a portion of the basement at the Star and Garter Hotel, would, with certain alterations, provide a suitable shelter. That recommendation was approved by the A.R.P. Committee who directed that immediate steps be taken to carry out the proposal.

The Surveyor suggested the adaptation where possible of suitable basements and caves and the erection of new type surface shelters. He advised shelters to hold not more than 50 people.

The Surveyor was authorised to proceed immediately with plans and estimates for 20 public shelters, each to hold 50 persons. The Surveyor was asked to obtain tentative approval from the Regional Technical Officer upon that proposal and also to seek the Officer's advice regarding the suitability of tunnelling. The Committee reported having received a deputation of Westcott residents who urged the Council to consider the possibilities of tunnelling in this district and to use initiative and determination in providing public shelters. Mr. Somner told the deputation that the Surveyor was making a detailed survey of the district's shelter needs and that the Council were actively considering the matter. He pointed out that there was a shortage of materials and that the more vulnerable areas had priority in the issue of available materials.

The Surveyor reported on a Home Security circular regarding

tunnelling. After consideration, the Committee was satisfied that nowhere in the district where a tunnelling scheme was prima facie justifiable would it be possible in view of the Ministry's stringent requirements.

The Surveyor stated that he had obtained an estimate for steel framed, wire mattressed double bunks, at 55s. each, or 50s. each if 200 were ordered. The A.R.P. sought approval for the fitting of bunks in all suitable existing shelters and in any future shelters provided in the district.

Subject to Regional approval, 150 two tier steel tubular bunks costing 41s. each are to be bought for public shelters.

The Surveyor was asked to inquire regarding the provision of low voltage wall heaters for public shelters.

Surface Shelters Criticised.

The Surveyor reported that he had placed a contract with Mr. G. Cornwell to provide wooden seating in the 17 communal shelters at a cost of £3.10s. per shelter. Confirming that action, the A.R.P. Committee decided that a back rail be included in the contract, the total cost not to exceed £4 per shelter.

Mr. Wilkinson questioned the wisdom of going to that expense. "I have inspected one of these shelters rather carefully", he said, "and it appears to me that, if a person has the average length legs, it will be impossible for him to sit in the wretched things." He complained of the bad design of the shelters and said he was certain, water, dripping from the roof, would soak through the brick walls. With slight additional expense, that could have been avoided. He described the construction of the shelters as "scandalous" and a "waste of public money".

Major Chance, speaking of "these unfortunate shelters" suggested that, to give the public a feeling of greater security, iron uprights and rounded roofs, something like a Dutch barn, should be provided. That would help to keep the shelters dry and would take the first shock of any bomb falling.

Miss Evans spoke of two shelters being full of water. Mr. Wilkinson said he understood that one local authority wanted to add "drip bricks" in the construction of the shelters, but the Regional Authorities said any additional expense incurred in building the shelters would have to come from the local rates. Yet it seemed to him that, if all the borough engineers throughout the country had protested against the design of the shelters, the Government would have been compelled to move. It was wrong for local authorities to take the thing "willy nilly" when they knew the Government's design for these shelters meant a waste of money.

Mr. Somner deplored any public statement that the shelters were not safe. He had been told by a reliable person who was in the

53

building trade that the smallness of the shelters was an asset. Practical men said the shelters were sound and, for their purpose, the design was good. Admittedly, the shelters were cramped in space but the bigger the shelter, the bigger was the target. The A.R.P. Committee had plans for roofing the gaps between the shelters (See photo of air raid shelter in Ashley Road, Westcott. This is the type being referred to) and for taking away the roof water so as to make the interior dry. Mr.Somner asked the Council to agree to the provision of seats in the shelters but he added: "I think it is safe to assure the Council that we shall not build any more of these shelters; we hope to get a much better design for the next twenty shelters". (The Ashley Road shelter was pulled down in 1941 and a flat roof design was built, of which the only one still standing in Westcott is at the school).

Concerning amenities in shelters and the control of shelters, the A.R.P. Committee reported having received a letter from Mr. J.G. Sandell. Dealing with points raised in the letter, the Committee decided that kettles should not be provided in public shelters.

Replying to Major Chance, Mr. Somner said ways would be tried to provide facilities for people to make themselves hot drinks while spending nights in the shelters. Many aged and infirm people as well as children spent nights in the shelters.

Major Chance was anxious that these people should have the means of making hot drinks. It was not suggested that the cost should fall on the rates; only that facilities should be provided.

At Major Chance's suggestion, a resolution was passed that hot water should be provided in the public shelters wherever possible and that the A.R.P. Committee should find the best means of doing that.

Mr. Somner reported that he had approached the local branch of the W.V.S. regarding the use of their mobile canteen to provide light refreshments at public air raid shelters at night, but it was not found practical to proceed with the proposal.

Terms suggested by Messrs. Montague Burton Ltd., having been accepted, the air conditioning plant at their High Street premises is to be adapted to serve the public basement shelter below those premises.

Disinfectant sprays are to be provided at wardens' posts and public air raid shelters.

School Shelters. A County Council letter set out the conditions which that Council felt bound to make respecting the public using school shelters.

The Dorking Council agreed to accept the County Council's

conditions and to enforce them as far as possible but they pointed out that they did not know of any authority to employ paid shelter marshals, as suggested in the County Council's letter.

Brockham had 28 new watchers. The Committee said they could not provide badges but would provide armlets bearing the letters "W.W."(Warden Watcher).

The A.R.P. officer reported the receipt of 29000 ear plugs for free distribution. It was decided that the plugs should be distributed through the warden's posts.

Mr. Teede remarked that at his post there had not so far been a single application for ear plugs.

A County Council letter, regarding the replacement of A.R.P. uniforms. It was resolved that the A.R.P. Officer show to the Committee the number of persons in the various A.R.P. services, the uniforms at present supplied, and on order, and the additional uniforms required.

One hundred and thirty water-proof coats costing 25s. each and 110 ground sheet capes, costing 12s. each, are to be bought for members of the outside A.R.P. services not already so equipped. Also 162 uniforms are to be bought at cost of about £99. An additional 30 sets of A.F.S. uniforms, making 80 sets on order, are to be obtained.

December 6/40   A crew of six Dorking firemen with their fire fighting appliances joined the big company of firemen who fought the fires caused at Southampton by enemy raids last Saturday and Sunday nights. The Dorking men had an exciting journey to Southampton during Sunday night. Near Guildford, an army lorry, unable to pull up quickly on the slightly icy road surface, crashed into the Dorking trailer pump, damaging it but not seriously affecting its pumping qualities. No one was hurt in the crash, and the firemen carried on. Reaching Southampton in the early hours of Monday morning, they were engaged first at a works fire, and then dealt with several small fires in a residential and commercial part of the City. They worked right throughout Monday, and did not leave Southampton until Tuesday morning. They returned to Dorking unshaven, unwashed, and weary but yet ready, after a night's rest, to tackle any new calls which might come.

December 13/40   Dorking W.V.S. Canteen. Noble work after Southampton raids. The experiences of four local residents - Mrs. Dumas and Mrs. Pritchard, of Brockham, and Mrs. Lindsay and Miss Dobinson - who took part in feeding and caring for those suffering injury, or whose homes had been destroyed in recent bombing raids on Southampton, were described in a talk by Mrs. Dumas.

Mrs. Dumas said their experiences began on Sunday evening, when

she was asked if she would lend her car and drive the Dorking
W.V.S. canteen trailer to Southampton. She at once agreed, and
enlisted the sympathy and help of Mrs. Pritchard. They set off
next morning with a heavy trailer packed with tea and supplies of
food. After a somewhat eventful journey, for their trailer was
overloaded, they reached Southampton and reported at their
appointed centre, where they found W.V.S., firemen, police,
A.R.P, and other canteens, making tea on gas rings or primus
stoves, and they at once joined in the good work. Many of the
people had had no sleep for three days and nights, and had been
feeding firemen and helpers who had come from many parts of
England.

That night the Dorking W.V.S. members slept in their motor rugs
in a hall, where the chairs were full of sleeping firemen and
police, until five next morning, when they got busy boiling water
and making tea and sandwiches until eight. They were then told
to go to a part of the city which had been bombed, and here they
spent the rest of the day till the light began to go. The
firemen there had been working since three in the morning, and
were grateful for the food and refreshment they were able to
provide them with. That night they tried to get beds at a
local"pub", but like all other similar places, it was full. They
then tried a Council house, and asked if they could have beds.
"Certainly", said the lady of the house, "We all sleep
downstairs, and you can have the beds upstairs". So they had a
comfortable night, and the people of the house would not take a
penny in payment.

That day they worked with a Corporation brazier and coke which
was given them. They "scrounged" around and got a supply of
bread and some currant cake. At 11 o'clock they went down to the
demolition squads. They found a soldier looking for his pal, but
he found his pal's gas mask only. They came across a girl
looking for her people. It was very sad. They afterwards went
to another part of the city but, after working there a short
time, had to leave. They then set up outside some insurance
offices and did their washing up on the steps. They served six
hundred cups of tea that day, and innumerable sandwiches. They
made no charge but, as some people wished to leave some
acknowledgment, they had a collecting box which realised 15s.

Ending this interesting talk, Mrs. Dumas advocated the
provision of a depot outside every town in England to help meet
such emergencies as those which came to Southampton. Mrs.
Pritchard, who added a few words to what Mrs. Dumas had
described, said that the morale of the people was excellent.
They would do anything they could to help one another, and the
police were admirable.

December 20/40   Four months ago, a silver haired lady in
Westcott thought that more might be done for members of the
Services. She talked over her idea with other ladies, and also
consulted the Chairman of the British Legion who, in turn,
consulted his Committee. The result was the forming of the

The Falkland Road Fountain c 1919.

See page 59

57

Services Club and Canteen, which occupied two rooms, one large and the other small, at the British Legion Hut. The large room is fitted with easy chairs, a piano, a gramophone, games and papers; the smaller is a quiet room with small tables, writing materials, and a library. Both rooms have been redecorated and have cheerfully coloured cushions and curtains to make them homelike. The kitchen has been fitted with a boiler, for the making of many cups of tea and coffee, and a large gas range, for the preparation of hot meals. A rota of some 60 of the fair sex take their turn, three or four on duty at a time, to run the canteen. And right at the beginning they were fortunate in securing a Secretary who possesses inexhaustible energy - Lady Touche. The committee consists of : Chairman Mrs. Eastham; Vice Chairman Mrs. Gooch and Mrs. Clinton; Hon. Sec. Lady Touche; Hon. Treasurer, Miss E.G. Moore; Mrs. Nicholson, Mrs. Etheridge and Miss Ryde. The members of the Services can use the three billiards tables of the Legion Club, the table tennis tables and darts boards. Two to three dances are held weekly in the large hall, when some 200 dancers are on the floor at a time. And the Canteen Committee is about to commence a series of concerts and entertainments in this hall in which there is a good stage. The club is doing great work, and all those concerned can be congratulated on making life easier for the Service men.

December 27/40   The crew of Dorking firemen, who took a tender and pump to Southampton to help in the firefighting there after the recent heavy enemy raid, have received a message of thanks from the Chief Officer of the Southampton Fire Brigade. "Your appliance", he writes, "in conjunction with those from other districts arrived promptly and rendered valuable assistance to my own Brigade. The town was faced with a crisis as severe as any that could have been anticipated, and it was only by the promptness of your men in carrying out their instructions and their splendid devotion to duty which prevented further terrible destruction. Lack of water and communication made their work very arduous and difficult. Please convey my thanks to all those men who so ably gave assistance."

January 3/41   Public Shelters, Westcott.

In Bailey Road on spare land opposite No.27; in Watson Road at the Northern end; on Westcott Green on a site to be agreed with the Lord of the Manor; in St. John's Road (disused pumping station to be adapted as a shelter). The Surveyor's action in ordering 100 three tier steel bunks at 53s. each was approved. The Westcott Siren. The A.R.P. Officer reported that an air raid warning siren had been installed at Westcott, but the volunteer wardens there were unable to man the warden's post continuously. It was decided to engage an additional paid warden for service in Westcott.

January 3/41   Once again the Dorking Fire Brigade have responded to a call for aid by a raid stricken city. Last Sunday night, a crew of Dorking A.F.S. men went to help in fire fighting in the City of London, and a lorry carrying a water tank also went from Dorking to the City. It was an arduous but thrilling trip.

January 10/41 The day following the appeal by the Home Secretary and Minister of Home Security to people to play their part in guarding their works, shops, business premises and homes against enemy fire raisers, arrangements were made for a part of Dorking High Street on the South side from Messrs. White and Sons' premises to Pump Corner - to be watched at night by voluntary fire spotters. Forty two people - shop owners, managers and male members of the staffs - have volunteered as spotters, and six are on duty each night with headquarters at the rear of Messrs. Stone and Turner's premises (now Sainsbury's). Their apparatus consists, at the moment of stirrup pumps and each trader or shop manager has been asked to see that there is a pail of sand and a pail of water on their premises at all times. It is expected that many other sections of the town will soon have their fire spotting schemes in operation.

Local residents will have noticed that sandbags marked "Fire", have been dotted around the streets of the district. These are for dealing with incendiary bombs. Should an incendiary bomb fall, someone should grab the sandbag and dump it on the bomb. Do not waste time by opening the sandbag and pouring out the sand. Throw it bodily on to the bomb. Then get a stirrup pump ready for action if necessary.

Jaunuary 17/41 Another call has come for more voluntary war service. To meet the threat of fire raising raids by enemy planes, fire watchers are urgently needed to patrol the streets so that incendiary bombs wherever they fall, may be smothered before they can cause big blazes. The ideal organisation at which to aim is one which provides fire watching patrols for every street every night. That will require many volunteers and the flow of volunteers for war work is slack. Yet there are still not a few men and women who are not doing much or even any voluntary war work. These people must now come forward for fire watching duties. The Government are issuing an Order making fire watching compulsory but the compulsion may not at first be enforced for residential areas and the less vulnerable areas. The Government's intention is that premises, particularly those which are unoccupied at night should not be left unwatched for any considerable length of time. A meeting was held at Dorking this week on this subject. The meeting decided that an organisation of fire watchers should be established in Dorking, based in its early stages, on the A.R.P. Wardens' service. The wardens and leaders of fire watching parties will during the next few days, be asking members of all households to volunteer for fire watching duties. Everyone is urged to respond willingly and to the limit of his or her ability.

January 31/41 Dorking Council. Falkland Road Fountain. The Highways Committee received a letter from Mr. S.J. Clear, stating that he had collided with the drinking fountain in Falkland Road, while driving his car at night. He considered that the fountain was insufficiently lighted. The Surveyor told the Committee that the fountain was adequately lighted at the time of the accident. However another warning lamp had been placed on the fountain and the base had been painted white.

Mr. Somner said motorists were told by the Ministry of Transport that a red light should be taken to be the offside rear light of a vehicle, so that when a motorist saw a red light, he swung right automatically to pass the suspected vehicle on the offside. If he did so when passing the red light on the Falkland Road fountain, he went to the wrong side of the road and placed himself in danger. Mr. Somner suggested that the fountain should be properly lighted with a white light.

Mr. Wilkinson:"Is there any sentimental reason why this lump of old iron (referring to the fountain) should remain there? Something better could be done with the space it occupies."

The Chairman said the question whether the fountain should be removed or not would have to be considered by the Committee.

Mr. F.W.G. Clinton (Westcott) has been appointed whole time paid warden.

February 14/41 and May 17/1985   Fire fighters had red faces
Sir: - The following is a report extracted from The "Dorking Advertiser" of February 14th 1941.

The heavy trailer pump at Milton Court.

Dorking firemen had a unique job on Friday 7th. Soon after mid-day they were called to a fire pump on fire. Messrs. W.T. Henley's Telegraph Works Ltd., have had a heavy trailer pump at Milton Court for fire protection work on their premises. Last Friday the pump's petrol tank was being filled, near the pump there was a heating lamp, the petrol caught fire and quickly the pump was enveloped in flames. The Dorking firemen flooded the pump with water from the first aid apparatus, but the pump was completely burnt as to be little more than a heap of scrap metal. A considerable amount of hose was also destroyed.

(I can well imagine the fire officer while waiting for the fire brigade to arrive rushing around in circles shouting "Don't panic, don't panic, don't panic".

A ready made script for the T.V series of "Dad's Army", surely?

D. Knight, Furlong Road, Westcott).

February 21/41 St. Martin's Dorking, Annual Church Meeting. Fire Watching. Mrs. White (Hon. Sec. of the Church Council) continued, fresh precautions against fire had been taken. Ladders had been erected and were permanently in position, so that every portion of the roof could be reached, and an ample supply of sand had been distributed around and about the church. Seven of their members were taking their part with fire watching squads, which included the church and church room in their area for watching. Mr. E.L. Sellick said he shuddered to think what some amateur members were likely to do on the ladders in the black out if ever they had occasion to get on the church roof. He hoped there was some understanding that only people who were skilled in the use of ladders should use them.

Mr. Pickford thought those who were likely to have to use the ladders should have some practice in their use.

March 7/41 Invest in Victory. Dorking War Weapons Week. An Exhibition.

As a side line for the War Weapons Week there has been an exhibition of war souvenirs and war photographs, held by the courtesy of the East Surrey Gas Company in the Company's showrooms in High street. It is a small exhibition, but remarkably interesting. There are numerous parts of German aeroplanes, some showing signs of the crash which was the finish of their career, and some showing signs of the flames following the crash. The exhibits include a German airman's helmet and parachute. There are several bombs of various sizes, part of a case containing incendiary bombs and a contraption labelled "Molotoff portmanteau". The photographs, which were supplied by the Ministry of Information, illustrate many aspects of the nation's war effort.

March 7/41 Whistles are wanted. They are wanted for the use of fire watchers. Whistles cannot be bought easily nowadays, so gifts are being sought from the public. Any whistle capable of producing short sharp blasts will do, possibly even the best of those toy whistles found in Christmas crackers, the whistles with which children make horrible noises at Christmas parties. Gifts of whistles will be gratefully received by the Dorking A.R.P. Officer.

March 14/41   Night raider down at Ockley. One of the German bombers which made widespread attacks over Britain on Wednesday night was brought down in flames at Ockley, a short distance from the Sussex border. It had, apparently, been successfully attacked by a night fighter. One of the crew baled out, was captured and taken to hospital, while the dead body of another, who also took to his parachute, was found by members of the Home Guard. Three other members of the crew were found dead in the crashed plane.

August 11/1978   Army Bomb Disposal experts gingerly defused a live thousand pound wartime bomb this week amid the wreckage of the German bomber, which has been found buried in an Ockley field.

But they warned sightseers especially children, to keep away. They believe three or four potentially deadly bombs still lie a few feet below the surface of the field, at Dene Farm on the county border.

The plane, now just fragments of rusty metal, is believed to be a Heinkel III shot down in 1941. Human bones, assumed to be those of the pilot and crew, have also been dug from the wreckage.

The plane was first located by the Air Historical Group. Working from historical records they established the plane had been shot down over the Dorking area in March 1941.

The owner of the land gave them three weeks to comb the area. With the aid of metal detectors they discovered wreckage buried in the field about 15 feet down.

The Army Bomb Disposal Squaa and the police were called in as soon as the live bomb and human bones were unearthed.

Now the Army have sealed off the area while excavation work goes on to find any remaining bombs.

The Army have to try to trace the identity of the human remains.

August 18/1978   The Army have sounded the "All Clear" at the Ockley field, where a thousand pound war time bomb was found in the wreckage of a crashed Nazi plane.

Army chiefs were worried that there might be more bombs in the field at Dene Farm. But after a thorough week long search of the area, the men are ready to pack up and move out.

The search for more bombs was conducted by following the flight path of the aircraft with metal detectors.

The defused bomb was taken away by the Army to be used as a C.D. training aid for young soldiers.

The wreckage of the aircraft is officially the property of the Ministry of Defence, but it will probably go to the finders. They intend to clean it up and put it on show in a museum.

An inquest is expected on the human remains - a leg and part of a pelvis - found in the plane. The Army are trying through war time records, to establish the identity of the pilot.

Effects found include a shoe and a French franc.

The owner of the farm is Mr. John Richardson, a pig breeder. He said:"The Army haven't been too much trouble really".

April 4/41 Dorking Bench. Windows broken by crowd.

An incident at Westcott was described by P.C.Hamilton in giving evidence against Mrs. B. of Heathcote, Main Road, Westcott, who was summoned for allowing an unscreened light to show from her house. The constable spoke of seeing a light shining from Heathcote, and finding that Mrs. B. was attending a concert at the British Legion Club, he sent for her there and she came immediately. In the meantime, however, people living in Furlong Road became annoyed and threw stones, breaking several panes of glass in the house. Aircraft were overhead at the time. Mrs. B. told the Bench that the light was showing from a spare room. The light switch in this room had become so loose that, when shutting the door with a bang, the light went on of its own accord. She was very sorry for the trouble caused. - Fined £2.

April 4/41 Our Readers' Views. The fire sandbags.Sir: - As a resident of Dorking, I am disgusted at the present state of the sandbags placed at the base of lamp posts in the town. From a hygienic point of view, could they not be tied about three to four feet up the lamp post, as I noticed has been done in another town.
Yours etc, "Observant".

April 4/41 Dorking Urban District Council. The A.R.P Committee considered complaints of the inaudibility of the Westcott siren. The A.R.P. officer and the Surveyor reported that they were satisfied that the siren was efficient and that any inaudibility must be due to the configuration of the Westcott area.

Mr. Somner said the A.R.P. Committee had never pretended that the Westcott siren was as audible as the Dorking sirens. A small siren was provided at Westcott because the amount of money available for it was restricted by the Regional Authority.

Pumping Well as a Shelter.

The proposal to adapt the disused pumping well at Westcott has received Regional approval.

Work on the adaptation of the pumping well at Westcott is to proceed at once Messrs. Preston and Habgood's tender being accepted.

A Surrey County Council letter stated that Council proposed to provide air raid shelters for 150 children at the Westcott School, and asked if the Dorking Council wanted the use of the shelters. The offer was accepted with thanks.

April 4/41 Hoping by personal example to make people conscious of the risk of poison gas being used, and particularly to get people to carry their gas masks. Councillor H.S. Woodward and his son, aged 9, wore their gas masks during a three quarters of an hour's walk on Tuesday afternoon. They went for a stroll in the Nower Road, Milton Heath and Westcott Road district, wearing their masks all the time. They heard from passers by several complimentary remarks - not about their personal appearance, but about the valuable lesson they were teaching. The writer of this note was in Dorking Fire Station on Tuesday. When a bell rang all the firemen on duty donned their gas masks immediately. Then they continued their work, wearing masks for some time. This it was learnt was part of a daily drill. On Wednesday morning, all the members of the staff at the Dorking Council Office at Pippbrook had a gas drill, wearing gas masks even while telephoning.

April 16/41 Eleven high explosive bombs fell from Coombe Farm to Deerleap Road, all failed to explode. The last fell in the garden of Miss M.P. Bronsdon, Durfold, Westcott. It was a 1100 lb. bomb.

June 20/41 Last week two of the Dorking A.R.P. women ambulance drivers went to Kingston. They stood for a while looking in a shop window. Then they found that they were crying and not because they wanted some frocks and dare not use their clothes coupons! Turning round, they saw that people in the street were wearing gas masks. A demonstration with tear gas was in progress. The ambulance drivers had left their gas masks in Dorking!

June 27/41 Shelter Warden. Mr. and Mrs. T.F. Gatford, St. John's Road, Westcott, for St. John's Road shelter. (This means this shelter was open by this date).

July 11/41 Loans of telescopes are required by the Home Guard. Anyone willing to make such a loan is asked to communicate with Major J.F. Somner at North Holmwood School House, or with Lieut. S.A. Moore at Charmiane, Deepdene Avenue, the signals officer,

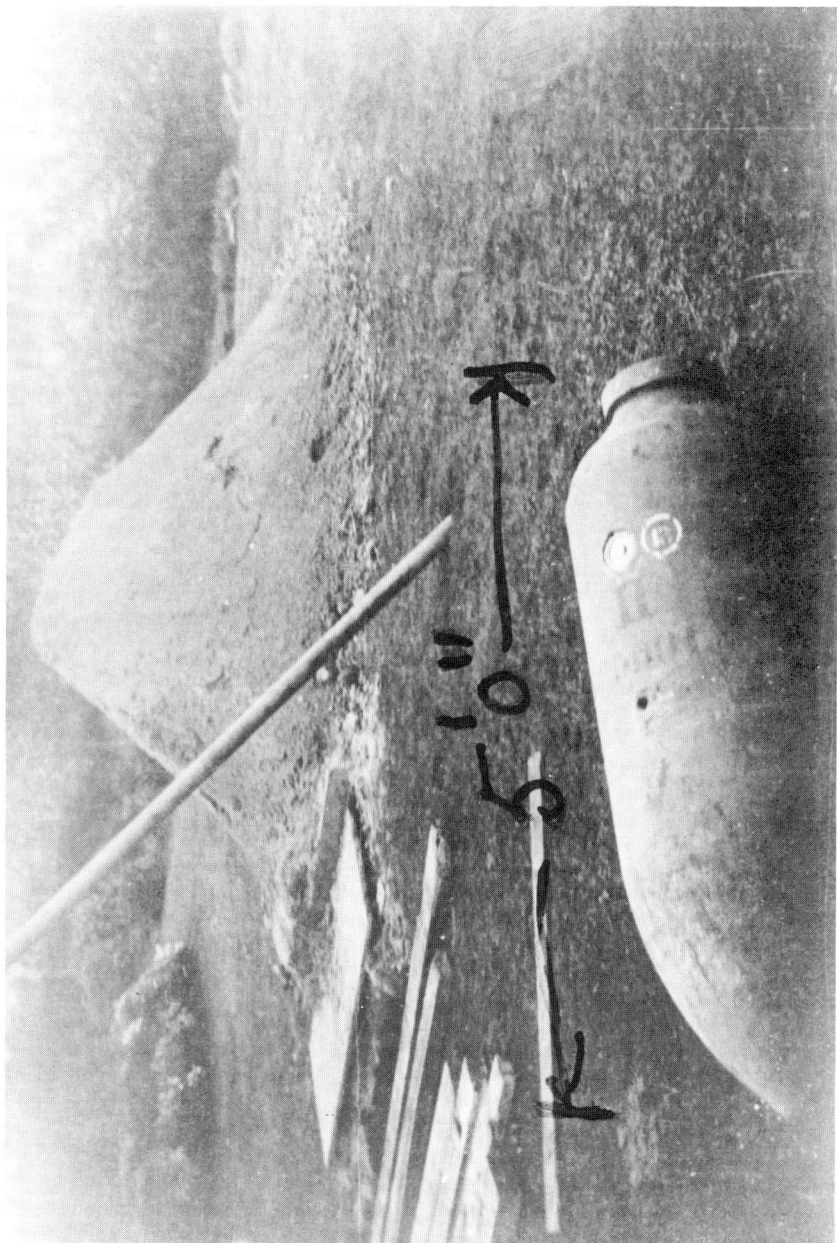

5' 0"

See page 64

The unexploded bomb in Deerleap Road, Westcott.

65

Canadian gift for Dorking. A mobile canteen.

See page 70

who is willing to give a personal guarantee that, as far as lies in his power, every possible care will be taken of loaned telescopes.
July 18/41 The Secretary of State for War, Capt. David Margeson, paid a brief visit to a Home Guard school in the South Eastern command on Monday morning. This Home Guard school is accommodated in a mansion on a lovely hilltop (Denbies Mansion).

August 1/41 D.U.D.C. matters. Only one little bomb please. The Highways Committee reported having considered the desirability of removing the drinking fountain in Falkland Road, but resolved to take no action in the matter.

Mr. Bell: "Is it possible to call the attention of Happy Hermann's Luftwaffe to this fountain?"
Mr. Kirk:"If they localise their bomb!"

August 8/41 During daylight hours one day next week - that is between today and Friday August 15th - there will be a liberation of tear gas in the town area of Dorking to test the civilian population's readiness to meet a gas attack and to act as an object lesson of the importance of carrying gas masks. Be prepared!

August 15/41 Where did the oranges go? Sir:- It was stated last week in the daily press that a large consignment of South African oranges were being distributed throughout the home counties in sufficient quantities to prevent the necessity for under-the-counter and back door sales. But though a consignment came into Dorking during the weekend, it appears that few, if any, were available for ordinary customers and none were on view.

Maybe, of course, the retailers in a burst of generosity gave them away quietly to the poor. On the other hand, the under-the -counter method of selling certain commodities having become such a habit, they quietly parcelled out the whole consignment amongst the favoured and the affluent.

If the latter explanation is the correct one, it will be interesting to see what action the Local Food Controller is going to take in the matter.
Yours etc, L.P. Brand, Heatherdene, Deepdene Gardens, Dorking.

August 15/41 The gas test in the town area of Dorking was postponed.

August 29/41 Schoolchildren to Harvest wild fruit crop.
The Board of Education in a memorandum issued to schools today urge the need for making the best possible use of the autumn wild fruit crop - blackberries, bilberries, crab apples, elderberries, rowan berries and sloes - which it is expected will amount in all to some thousands of tons. - Fruit collected by schools can, if not used for immediate consumption, be sold to fruit preservation centres or made into jam by the schools for their own consumption; additional supplies of sugar will be available to

schools for this purpose from the local Food Offices. Advice on picking the fruit, and warnings to avoid damage to crops, and to obtain the permission in advance of the owners of the land are given.

September 19/41   The Dorking Technical Institute is running a non stop programme of evening classes this year. For the first time, there has been a summer session as well as the normal winter session. The Institute has continued its good work throughout the year in spite of air raids and blackout. Even when bombs have fallen near by, it has carried on; for it can now be stated - long after the event that, one night last winter, a bomb fell within a few yards of the Institute building (November 1st.1940). The evening classes have attracted many soldiers, who are keen on learning German and French. One soldier, asked why he was learning German said "Well, we are going to Berlin one day!"

September 19/41   Beginning last Saturday and Sunday afternoons, and continuing during the evenings of this week, a car fitted with a loud speaker has been touring Dorking streets delivering the following message loudly and distinctly:- "Calling all, calling all. This is the Warden Service calling. Have you looked at your blackout before you switch on your lights? Are you sure no light is showing from your rooms at night? Go outside and inspect, you cannot see from the inside. You have been warned; it may be costly if you fail to carry this out. Have you tried on your gas mask lately? Do you ever put it on at all? Hitler will not tell you when he is coming. Be prepared, be prepared. What about your stirrup pump - use it at least once a week. Have you water close at hand for the Fire Guard? And are you going to help them when they help you? Contact your Warden and make a note of his address. Do you know what to do if fire bombs fall on your home, in your garden, or road? They may burn your home if not tackled at once. Don't forget to clear that junk from your loft. Don't forget Fire Bomb Fritz will come again. Will you put him out? Don't forget your watchword, "Britain shall not burn". In the last war we said "Keep the home fires burning" - now we say, "Go to it and put them out".

September 19/41   Six hundred Morrison shelters have been received in Dorking for distribution to householders throughout the urban district. So far, 109 have been issued free and eight or nine have been purchased by householders at £7 each. The shelters of which a specimen has been erected in Dorking Market Place, are six feet by four feet, heavy steel construction. When erected, they can be used - while not required as air raid shelters - as a table. A booklet is issued with each shelter explaining the simple methods of erection. The shelters are available for free issue to householders whose income does not exceed £350 a year; in a household with more than two children of school age, the limit of £350 may be increased by £50 for each child in excess of two.

September 21/41   a British plane crashed near Dorking Town

Station just North of the railway line.
[From A.R.P. Map of Dorking].

October 3/41   Gas Exercises.   The A.R.P Committee's report
contained references to the holding of a tear gas test in Dorking
town. Mr. Kirk asked the Council to go steady with gas exercises.
Several cases were pending of claims against certain Corporations
who had held gas exercises. There was no authorisation, as far
as he knew, for local authorities releasing gas in the streets.

The Chairman said the Council acted under the instructions of
the Region in this matter. The Government was spending thousands
of pounds in publicity to get people to carry gas masks, and they
had given instructions to local authorities and had supplied gas
generators.

Mr. Kirk: "I don't think you have instructions to release tear
gas".
The Chairman: "We have instructions to have exercises".

Mr. Trim hoped that, in future gas exercises, if any
postponement was necessary, the exercise would take place as
quickly as possible after the postponement. He was told by
tradesmen that the delay after the postponement of the last
exercise had an adverse effect on local trade because people, and
especially elderly people did not care to come into town while
there was a risk of a gas exercise being held.

Loud Speaker Propaganda.   The A.R.P. Committee recorded
appreciation of the Civil Defence propaganda work recently done
by the Deputy Chief Warden through a loud speaker tour of the
district.

The Chairman said he had received numerous commendations from
the public, but he had also received one letter of very strong
criticism about the use of loud speakers at 3 o'clock on a Sunday
afternoon. This writer felt that time was very ill-chosen.

October 24/41   How will the residents of Dorking take to the
idea of an occasional hour of music on their spare afternoons?
To discover the answer to this question, well known professional
musicians of Dorking and the neighbourhood have decided to
experiment with an "informal hour and music" on Wednesday
afternoons. October 29th, November 26th and December 17th. The
music will last from 3 to about 4 p.m. at the White Horse
Assembly Rooms. Admission will be 1s. payable at the doors. Mr.
William Murdoch, the famous pianist, has kindly offered to
inaugurate the series by playing at the first concert. At the
second concert, Miss Ivy Herbert, whose lecture recitals have
been so successful, will be the pianist, the singer will be our
popular Dorking baritone, Mr. S. Arthur Andrews, and last but not
least, the songs will be accompanied by Dr. William Cole, Miss
Vera Kantrovitch, leader of the Women's String Orchestra, will
play violin sonatas at the third concert with Mr. Eric Gritton, a
musician whose name needs no recommendation to Dorking audiences.

There will be no formal programme, but the music will be briefly "annotated" by Dr. Vaughan Williams and other speakers. Mr. Murdoch has agreed to act as "compere" to his own recital. It is hoped that, if these informal music makings are successful, they will be continued in the New Year. It remains to be discovered what day and hour will be most popular. What about a series of "lunch hour" concerts on the lines of the National Gallery concerts?

November 21/41 Canadian gift for Dorking. A mobile canteen, provided by the Women's Club of Montreal, Canada, has been presented to Dorking. It was accepted, on Dorking's behalf last Thursday by the Chairman of the U.D.C.

This useful gift has come to Dorking through the influence of Mrs. L. Archer, of Courtlands, Deepdene Avenue, Dorking, who has Canadian associations. It is a compact and neatly arranged van in which hot drinks can be prepared and from which light refreshments can be served. It is intended, primarily, for use in this district and chiefly, of course, to provide immediate meals for persons requiring such help if this district were bombed. But it will also be ready to answer regional calls for help in heavily raided towns. The Dorking Women's Voluntary Services have accepted responsibility for staffing the canteen.

December 5/41 A man riding a cycle on Coast Hill, Westcott, was crushed and killed instantly by being struck by a 25 pounder gun - towed by a tractor - which was coming down the hill. After passing the cyclist, the tractor crashed into a private car, but although the car was wrecked, the two occupants escaped with severe bruises and cuts.

December 12/41 The British Restaurant, established by the D.U.D.C. at the former billiards hall in Junction Road, will be opened by Mr. Gordon Touche, M.P, at 11.45 a.m. next Thursday. The public are invited to attend that opening ceremony. Beginning next Thursday the restaurant will be open daily excepting Sundays from noon to 2 p.m. The price list will be: Two-course meal (meat with two vegetables and sweet), 11d.; meat course only (with two veg), 9d; sweet 2d; cup of tea or soup, 1d. Bread will be supplied free with meat meals. Children, if accompanied by adults, will be supplied with a two course meal for 6d. The restaurant has seating accommodation for 260 persons, and it is expected that from 500 to 700 meals can be served in the two hours of opening each day. Volunteer workers will be welcomed. The establishment of British Restaurants is in accordance with the Ministry of Foods national policy of providing all towns with an organisation ready to feed the public in case of heavy raids.

December 12/41 When Dorking British Legion members were out collecting gifts for the gift sale for the Aid to Russia effort, they came across a local clergyman well known to them. "We want something for our gift sale" said the Legion men. "Well, I've nothing at the Vicarage", replied the clergyman. And then, after a moment's pause, he added "Here, you had better take this" and he took off his overcoat, gave it to them and walked away coatless.

Here is another story from the gift sale. Among the gifts for sale at the South Street shop was a bird cage. Seeing it, a lady suggested it would sell better with a canary inside. She went out and returned a little later with a gift of a canary. At the auction the bird and cage fetched 22s.6d.

<u>December 26/41</u> Leave those strange objects alone.

Members of the public are again reminded that if they find any objects that appear to have been dropped from the air or washed up from the sea they should lose no time in telling the police or a warden. On no account should they touch them themselves.

Many attempts by individuals to move strange objects found on the land, or the beach, have had fatal results.

Fragments of bombs, goggles, diaries, bits of wireless apparatus, and other things, that look as if they have dropped from Nazi planes must not be kept as souvenirs. They are to be handed over to the police.

It is an offence under Defence Regulations 79 to keep in one's possession any article which there is reasonable cause to think has been dropped from an aircraft, or has formed part of a plane or of the arms, equipment or clothing carried by the crew. This includes unexploded incendiary bombs.

Heavy penalties can be imposed, and a number of people have already been convicted of this offence.

<u>January 2/42</u> The Falkland Road Fountain. The Council decided to consider in Committee a proposal that the fountain in Falkland Road should be removed and the resultant scrap metal made available to the Ministry of Supply.

Mr. Bell (Councillor) referred to the fountain as "that shrine of Victorianism". It was no longer used for its original purpose - a drinking fountain for horses - and now a Council workman had to go there with a lorry each night to put a lamp on the fountain, and a man had to go each morning to take the lamp away.

<u>January 2/42</u> Damage to shelters.

The A.R.P. Committee reported that locks and keys were to be provided for the doors of the new air raid shelters, and that the shelters would be kept locked when not in use.

Mr. N.G. Wilkinson (Councillor) explained that instances of damage being done in shelters had occurred. He hoped that anyone seeing such damage being done would report the matter.

Morrison Shelters. It was reported that 261 Morrison shelters had been delivered, and that only four applications were outstanding.

February 13/42 Soap Rationing. Each of the four coupons which make up a four weeks ration will entitle you to any one of the following: - either 4 oz. Hard Soap (common household soap in bars or pieces) or 3 oz. toilet soap or 3 oz. soap flakes or chips or 6 oz. soap powder No. 1 or 12 oz. soap powder No. 2 or 6 oz. soft soap. (From an advert issued by Ministry of Food).

February 20/42 The list published on Tuesday of Army awards in recognition of gallantry in carrying out hazardous work in a very brave manner includes the name of Lieut M.A. Clinton, R.E. who has been awarded the George Cross. Lt. Clinton is the son of Mr. F.W.G. Clinton of Coast Hill Cottage, Westcott, who is District Commissioner of Boy Scouts in the Dorking district and Deputy Chief Warden for A.R.P. Lt. Clinton has been engaged on bomb disposal work, but his parents do not yet know for what action the award of the George Cross has been made.

March 13/42 "Evans of the Broke" at Dorking. Admiral Sir Edward Evans visited Dorking on Monday; he and Lady Evans were the guests of Capt. C.D. Schermuly, at lunch at the Burford Bridge Hotel.

After visiting the Pippbrook Council offices, where he met the Chairman, members and officials of the Urban Council, Admiral Evans made a tour of inspection of the Warship Week selling centres. Then he went to the Embassy Theatre, where he was received by a very smart guard of honour provided by Sea Cadets from Reigate with their band.

March 20/42 Oranges now available. Fresh supplies of oranges are now available in the shops in Redhill, Reigate, Dorking, Godstone and district, and will be reserved for a period of five days, from yesterday, for issue at the rate of 1 lb. per head to children in possession of the green ration book.

After the five days reservation period has elapsed, surplus oranges may be sold to other customers, but retailers are asked to give priority to children, schools, hospitals and invalids.

April 3/42 More wilful damage. Mr. Wilkinson, Chairman of the A.R.P Committee, spoke strongly about damage being done at shelters after he had stated that the key of the emergency exit of a shelter below Messrs. Quicks was missing. Equipment and utensils in the shelters had been damaged or taken and doors had been broken open. He described the conduct of the persons responsible as "filthy", and said it made one wonder whether these people were worth providing shelters for. He asked that anyone knowing anything about damage being done would report to the police.

May 1/42 A military gun-towing vehicle which was drawing a gun weighing eight tons, was going down the steep hill from Ranmore Common into Dorking, when the brakes failed. The vehicle overturned, one of the soldiers was killed instantly, and three of the soldiers riding in the vehicle were injured.

May 6/42 the ammunition dump at Friday Street blew up. It was caused by a bush fire. People in Friday Street were evacuated.

January 28/1955 Mines and Bombs. 250 found at Leith Hill. "This is a warning to the public that there may still be unexploded anti-personnel mines and small bombs in the Leylands area of Leith Hill. These may have been left by the Military who were there during the war or they may be relics of the big fire which occurred in the summer of 1942 at an ammunition dump covering many acres between Friday Street and Leylands. In that fire a lot of ammunition was scattered by explosions. Last month, some old mines and bombs were found near the road leading from Leylands Farm to the Broadmoor-Friday Street junction. Since then a party of Royal Engineers have been "sweeping" with detectors the land at both sides of the road for about a third of a mile.

They have found about 250 mines and small bombs. Although it is thought that the area is now almost free of danger, there remains the possibility of a few odd bombs or mines being still buried".

May 8/42 Dorking and H.M.S. Titania.
Official contact through the Admiralty has now been made between Dorking and H.M.S. Titania, the submarine depot ship which this district has adopted as a result of its successful Warship Week effort in the National Savings campaign. Steps are being taken by the Admiralty for a replica of the ship's badge to be presented to Dorking and the D.U.D.C. will, it is expected, return the compliment by presenting to the ship a plaque commemorating the town's association with H.M.S. Titania.

May 8/42 The King visits Armoured Division.
Troops inspected on village greens and commons. One of the British Army's great Armoured Divisions was seen by His Majesty the King during a seven hour tour of part of the South-Eastern Command, which he made on Friday, when he inspected the units scattered over a wide area.

The King, who wore the uniform of a Field-Marshal, made his first call at a rugger pitch nestling at the foot of a hill, which is a famous beauty spot of the South country. (Boxhill and Pixham sports ground). The goal posts were still in position, and between them, round three sides of the pitch, were lined the troops, the sombre khaki of their battledress relieved by a thin line of black down one side of the formation - the berets worn by the men of a tank unit. Nearby, from the drive of a large house, a small group of civilians and several officers, watched the proceedings with interest, two other spectators watched from the top of the hill, probably unaware of the identity of the

73

inspecting officer, or of the discussion they were provoking. They were sharply silhouetted against the sky line, a fact that led to discussion between officers and war correspondents as to the range at which fire could be opened on such a perfect target!

From there the Royal procession travelled along country roads to a meadow in the grounds of a famous house associated with the memory of a well known English diarist,(John Evelyn and Wotton House) where his inspection of the troops was watched with keenness and evident enjoyment by village schoolchildren sitting in a row along the top of a stone wall. A common, set amid some characteristic English country scenery, with a distant background of wooded hills, was the setting for the King's next inspection, which was watched by a few villagers from the gardens of their cottages and a few more waiting for a bus almost opposite the point where the King alighted from his car.

News of the King's coming had evidently preceded him to the next place of call, for quite a number of people lined the boundaries of the triangular village green on whose smoothly mown cricket ground (Brockham Green) the units were drawn up in perfect formation. There were many children among the crowd which added a fourth spontaneous cheer, to the three rousing cheers which the soldiers, here as at the other places of call, gave His Majesty.

Divisional headquarters, where the King had lunch, came next, a famous country house whose tree-girt lawns, dotted with clumps of daffodils and spring flowers, made an unusual setting for the inspection. After lunch the King continued his strenuous tour.

May 15/42 Civil Defence Instructions.
An audience of nearly 900 crowded the Pavilion Cinema last Sunday morning to see two Civil Defence instruction films - one called "U.X.B", concerning bombs, and the other showing the correct ways of dealing with incendiary bombs and small fires. Those attending included the Home Guard, the A.T.C, the Women's Junior Air Corps, the wardens, and other A.R.P. services, fire guards, and firemen. Some of the contingents marched to the cinema. People who were there, or who saw the contingents arriving, were particularly impressed with the smart bearing of the Women's Junior Air Corps. This already large unit of girls, which has been in existence for only a month, marched with the precision of well trained soldiers. It was their first public appearance, and they were out to show that they had quickly and thoroughly learnt discipline, the first lesson in all the Services.

May 22/42 Mock Battle but real ammunition. The King sees his army being toughened. Attack on a Surrey Hill.

The toughening of the new reorganised British Army is a process that is gathering momentum visibly. In the course of many visits to military training centres in recent months (writes a special correspondent) I have noticed the process taking effect. The

74

British soldier who came out of Dunkirk was a grand fellow, even in temporary defeat; the British soldier who will one day return to the now enemy occupied continent will be even grander, a tough proposition with sinews of steel tempered by months of strenuous training under conditions approximating to those of the actual battlefield.

An exercise which was part of the process was witnessed by the King during visits which he paid to unit of an infantry division in the South Eastern Command on Thursday last week.(This was at Betchworth Lime works.) In this, a mock battle in which troops stormed a wooded height, live ammunition was used in the bombardment which covered the attack against an imaginary enemy holding the heights. Such exercises are not without their risks, but the men take them as a matter of course. There were two actual casualties in this battle, one man having a foot badly damaged when he trod on an unexploded grenade, and another receiving splinters in both arms from another explosion. I saw the former going into the ambulance and the latter coming away from the dressing station, and both were stoics in the true sense of the word.

The setting was a typical Surrey chalkpit with its background of chalk cliff, perpendicular in some places,slightly sloping in others where the accumulated scree offered a precarious foothold. To the right of the shrub topped hillock on which the war correspondents were accommodated, the King with officers of the unit stood on a high vantage point. On the left the ground sloped up from our mound and swept round in a semicircular curve to join the green wooded vista that topped the greyish white chalk face opposite us.

Scaling Difficult heights. Below us a thin line of khaki-clad figures, lightly clad - stripped for action as it were - advanced along the foot of the cliff. They were crouching with rifles and Bren guns ready, and an officer with drawn revolver led them. They started to scale the shallower cliff face to the right of the main position. It was difficult enough getting a foothold on the treacherous scree, but the advance party did it and crawled over the lip of the escarpment. Below them other khaki lines were filing along towards the steeper faces. Up to now the operation had been silent, but a distant rattle of machine gun fire presumably indicated that the imaginary holders of the hill top had spotted something. Through the swish of the rifle fire from the advance party broke the distinctive note of their Bren guns, and from behind us came the bang of a 2 in. mortar, followed by others. Puffs of dirty grey smoke half way up the hill preluded the ear splitting cracks of the projectiles. Now the ominous stutter of heavy machine guns cut in from shrubs close to our hillock, nearly deafening us. Soon the hillside was dotted with puffs of smoke as 3 in. mortars started laying a screen. The dirty grey line of the 2 in. mortars' explosives was moving upwards as the range lengthened.

Meanwhile the second khaki line below us had broken into small

75

groups of men, well spread out, who were storming the steeper heights, seeking a foothold here and there on the loose chalk, holding now to some cliff-face growth, now feeling for the edge where the green slopes began. Some dropped their rifles, threw up their arms and rolled realistically down the easier gradients as "casualties". Others pulled themselves up over the lip, flopped into the prone position and soon added their rifle and Bren gun fire to the din of the battle. To our left, in the bend of the curve, a party of sappers had scaled that part of the pit with ropes, and now a running-line was hauling up anti-tank guns, mortars and heavy equipment. Fresh detachments of infantry used another line to pull themselves up the steepest ascent and were dropping over the top to increase the fire power of the attack and to flank the defences.

The smoke screen was now enveloping the hill-top, and the thin khaki line stretched across the green slopes was moving up - a run, a jerk, a flop-down, another run, and so on. The covering fire, the attackers' fire, and the detonation of hand-grenades were blending into a devil's tattoo that echoed along the hills and seemed to throb back. Then most of the khaki line disappeared into the smoke haze and the covering fire began to ease up. Just as we left our vantage point the "success" signal flashed over our heads like a streak of fire. The attackers had taken their hilltop.

Earlier in the day the King had visited other units; among them a detachment of the "Queens", and had seen machine-gun training in full swing, new physical training that was part of the toughening process, advance field training, and many other phases of the Army's preparations.

At one place, where a chalkpit was again the setting, he watched men taking a "blitz" course - advancing over difficult ground with actual machine gun fire whistling just overhead and small explosives bursting on either side of the line of their advance. Their instructors, running ahead, drew them on with calls of "Hurry, hurry, get that Bosche before he gets you", and similar injunctions. After dropping behind cover to wipe out a Bosche "nest" with concentrated rifle fire, they continued their advance up the chalk slopes and disappeared over the top into a wood, while their instructors dropped back to fetch the next "blitz" squad over the same course.

Elsewhere the King watched massed rifle and Bren gun fire being directed on hillside targets, saw 2 in. and 3 in. mortars in action, as well as bigger artillery, and watched anti-tank guns being hauled into position, man-handled, put into action, and hauled away again.

May 29/42 Morrison Shelters do their job.
The A.R.P. Committee reported on an extended peiod for the distribution of Morrison shelters, and Mr. Wilkinson praised the efficiency of these shelters. He referred to an official statement that, in 24 houses which were completely demolished in

air raids, there were 119 persons in Morrison shelters. Although these shelters were not expected to take the weight of debris from a completely demolished house, yet, in these cases, only four of the 119 persons were killed. He advised those people who had room for a Morrison shelter, and who had not obtained one, to apply for one.

May 29/42 The boy scouts have started war service patrols in the town. These patrols are open to lads of 15 to 18 years of age, and they learn campaigning, signalling, exploring, patrolling, A.R.P, first aid etc. The War Office recognises these patrols as valuable pre-service training, exempting members from joining any other youth movement. Those interested, who need not have been scouts before, should apply at the Imperial Services Club, West Street.

June 12/42 H.M.S. Westcott is Westcott's adopted ship. One of the ship's officers, acknowledging two boxes of games, books and gramophone records, has written: "It was very kind indeed of you and of all the others at Westcott who collected together that grand lot of gramophone records and games. All the lads are very grateful, and told me to thank you personally for all of them. We are not a big ship as I expect you know. There are about one hundred and fifty sailors and eight officers. You may have seen in the papers some weeks ago that we sank a submarine, for which the captain was awarded the D.S.O, and several of the men the D.S.M. It was a great encouragement to everyone, and we are looking forward eagerly to our next catch.... We all thank you tremendously for your very kind presents, which I assure you we appreciate immensely". Westcott has now collected more games and records to be sent to the ship, and also a football (for which the ship's company specially asked) given by the children of the Sunday School.

September 25/42 The list of honours and awards announced this week in connection with the recent Malta convoy battle includes the names of officers and ratings of H.M.S. Westcott. It is inspiring to learn that the ship is carrying the name of Westcott in such a grand piece of heroic work as taking supplies to the brave defenders of Malta.

October 2/42 Boys find a "souvenir". One killed, two injured in explosion.

On Sunday, four Brixton boys came by train to Dorking for a day in the nearby country. During the day, they wandered into a chalkpit, where, in the past, military exercises have taken place. They were looking for souvenirs. They found one. Probably it was a grenade. The "souvenir" exploded, severely injuring three of the boys. The injuries to one of the boys proved fatal.

October 2/42 The removal of railings will commence at Caterham and Warlingham, and Dorking, on or after October 5th.

77

October 2/42   Phosphorus Bombs: The A.R.P. Committee and the Fire Staff Officer reported that he had arranged to distribute a solution to wardens for first aid treatment of burns which might be encountered should the new phosphorus bombs be used in this area.

Westcott, Ashley Road Air Raid Shelter.   *See page 45*

Miss Evans (Councillor) wanted the public to be told of the simple first aid treatment which she understood, was used for phosphorus burns.

Mr. Wilkinson (Councillor) said an application of bicarbonate was a simple and effective remedy.

October 30/42   Appeal to Westcott Residents.   The Deputy Surveyor told the A.R.P. Committee that at a public shelter in St. John's Road, Westcott, the exit door had been forced off and rain had entered the shelter, the ventilator case had been damaged, the landing at the bottom of the stairs had been fouled, rubbish had been thrown into the shelter, and a cupboard had been forced open.   The Committee decided to write to residents in the road telling them of the damage and soliciting their help in preventing future damage.

October 30/42   The Stand Easy canteen in West Street, Dorking, where grand work has been done for many months in supplying tea, coffee and light refreshments in congenial surroundings to Service men, is in need of three small carpets or rugs to replace some worn out by the boots of many soldiers.   If any of our readers can supply this need in part or in full, the canteen organisers will be grateful, and something more will have been done to bring a touch of home comforts into the lives of our Troops.

December 4/42   Royal Visit to Canadians.
The Princess Royal spent the day with Canadian military forces in the Home Counties area on Wednesday and following an inspection of one unit of which she is Colonel-in-Chief, watched the men in combined exercises.

Accompanied by Miss Sybil Kenyon-Slaney as Lady-in-waiting, Her Royal Highness was received by representatives of the Colonel Commandant of the Unit concerned, and a Brigadier.   She then inspected the Unit which was drawn up on a Recreation Ground. (Was this Pixham Sports Ground?)   The inspection was very thorough, and took over half an hour.   The Princess Royal then took her place at the saluting base outside the ground and the Unit marched past.

The Chairman of the local Council and his wife had the honour of being introduced to the Princess Royal.

The party then left for another part of the district, where combined exercises were held, in which every part of the modern Army together with the R.A.F. participated.

December 4/42   At a Dorking inquest on Friday the Coroner asked the "Dorking Advertiser" to bring to public notice a case in which a well-disposed person might show practical gratitude to a Good Samaritan. The inquest concerned the death of a London boy killed by a bomb taken as a souvenir while searching a place in which they should not have gone. Three of the boys had ghastly lacerated wounds. Mrs. Elsie King, who lives in a bungalow near the bombing range, told the Coroner that the uninjured boy ran to her bungalow for aid. She took towels and sheets to make bandages and tourniquets for first aid. At the end of her evidence the Coroner asked:"What about your towels and sheets?" Mrs. King replied that she did not at the time begrudge using them and, in similar circumstances, she would use her household linen again, but in view of the shortage of supplies and of coupons being required for towels she would like the articles replaced. She mentioned that, on two previous occasions when there had been accidents to soldiers in the bombing range, she had given articles of household linen for first aid dressings. Since the inquest we have spoken to the Food Office and the Citizens' Advice Bureau, and we learn that steps are being taken to give Mrs.King coupons with which to replace the towels. That, however, will not recompense her financially nor will it overcome the difficulty of getting new sheets now that supplies are short.

*   *   *

<u>January 22/43</u> German Plane Down, Enemy Pilot Captured.
A Focke-Wolfe 190 fighter bomber crash-landed in a ploughed field in the village of Capel a few minutes after one o'clock on Wednesday. After the plane hit the ground it ran into a hedge at the side of the field. The pilot was thrown clear, sustaining only minor scratches.

The plane caught fire and burnt fiercely. To villagers who were running towards it the German made a sign that they should stop and crouch down, a warning that was given just in time because explosions of the petrol tank and ammunition quickly made what an eyewitness described as "a fine display of fireworks". Some of the people who went towards the plane were blown over by the force of explosions. The plane was completely burnt out.

In the meantime the German pilot had been taken into custody. He walked away from the plane across the field into a garden, where he was met first by two brothers, Messrs. P.F. and W.A. Teasdale, local grocers, who with their van, were delivering goods to nearby houses. To Mr. Percy Teasdale he spoke in familiar French phrases, and Mr. Teasdale, with memories of the French he learnt in France during the last war, understood him. The pilot said he was "tout seul", and he also remarked:"La guerre est fini pour moi".

The brothers told him to come with them, and he meekly obeyed. They took him to the road where they met P.C. Cooper who was hurrying from his home, only a few hundred yards from the scene of the crash. Within an hour the German had been taken to Dorking police station and handed over to the military.

80

It is not known whether the plane was brought down by anti-aircraft fire or through damage received in a combat with a British fighter.

February 19/43 In view of the enemy's new air raid tactics of "tip and run" attacks on towns lacking military objectives, the D.U.D.C. have issued instructions that the air raid shelters in the town and some of the shelters in the villages shall be opened in the daytime. During the long period when air raids were infrequent, the shelters have been locked and the keys left in the custody of the nearest wardens. The decision to lock the shelters was made because many instances occurred of deliberate damage and theft being committed in the shelters. Unfortunately, with the reopening of the shelters, damage and theft recurred. Seats have been broken and electric light bulbs have been smashed or stolen. However, for the public's safety, the policy of keeping the shelters open is being maintained. The public, finding the shelters in darkness and with internal fittings damaged, must not blame the authorities, but the few senseless people whose actions cannot be too strongly condemned. Sometime one of the marauders will be caught and he will be, we hope, heavily punished.

March 12/43 Official notice has been given that the work of removing railings, scheduled as being unnecessary now and needed for war munitions, in the Dorking urban area, will begin on Monday next. The work will be done by a Ministry of Works gang, misnamed (for this job at least) "The Special Repair Service".

June 4/43 Mr. Leslie Howard, passenger in lost plane.
Mr. Leslie Howard, the film actor and producer, was one of the thirteen passengers on the civil plane lost on Tuesday while flying from Lisbon to this country. The plane left Lisbon at 9.30 on Tuesday morning. An hour and a half later, while over the Bay of Biscay, the wireless operator signalled "Enemy aircraft attacking us". That was the last heard of the plane.

The grief with which this news has been received by cinema devotees throughout the British Empire and America has been deepened for Dorking people because they knew Leslie Howard as a neighbour and friend. He lived at Stowe Maries, a picturesque house on the outskirts of Westcott. Although Mr. Howard's film work often kept him away from Westcott, he returned there whenever he could to spend quiet, happy days with polo ponies and in country pursuits. On several occasions in the happier days of peace, Mr. Howard helped in local affairs by opening fetes and by speaking at local gatherings. He was as charming at these affairs as he was on the screen.

He loved the Dorking countryside. Once addressing the Dorking Rotary Club, he echoed the call of another eminent Dorking resident, Dr. Vaughan Williams, that Dorking might become a centre of culture and the arts. Leslie Howard thought the Dorking neighbourhood could be an ideal place for film work.

Born in London on April 24th 1893, his name was Leslie Stainer until he took the stage name of Howard. When at Dulwich College he had written school plays and acted in them, and after joining the army on August 4th 1914, he took part in war-time theatricals in France. Upon being discharged from the Army he went on tour as a professional. He quickly reached the London stage, and then followed success after success in London and New York. His screen career began in 1930, and was marked by many artistic triumphs. The epic "Gone with the Wind" was one of his triumphs where he played the part of Ashley Wilkes.

In April last he went to Lisbon at the invitation of the British Council to deliver lectures in Portugal and Spain. His mission was extremely successful in both countries. As one result, 900 cinemas in Spain have agreed to show British documentary films. He illustrated his lectures with the film in which he starred "Pimpernel Smith", the story of a professor who helped refugees to escape from Germany.

He had intended to return to England last week, but postponed his journey so as to be present at the showing in Lisbon of the film "The First of the Few". The work in England upon which he was last engaged was supervising the final stages of his newest film "The Lamp Still Burns".

Deep sympathy is felt with Mrs. Howard and the son and daughter in their anxiety. His son, Ronald, now in the Navy, used to play for the Westcott Cricket Club.

June 4/43 The ancient annual event. The Fair which has been kept up for centuries, came to Dorking again this week. For two days, Wednesday and Thursday, it attracted large crowds of people trying to forget the war, if only for a few hours. Despite war-time conditions and petrol restrictions, the Fair, if considerably smaller than in peace time, was still remarkably large considering the handicaps to be overcome. In one direction at least however, the war has proved to be of assistance to the Fair. That is the introduction of Double Summer Time. Through this, the public is able to enjoy the amusements until nearly 11 p.m. without artificial lighting.

The war cannot stop Dorking Fair. It has lasted for hundreds of years. May it last for hundreds more!

June 11/43 Iron railings are disappearing to make munitions. In many instances, the removal of the railings has improved the appearance of buildings. We like the view of St.Martin's Church better now that most of the cold, ugly iron along the footpaths has been taken. Certainly the approach to the Dorking Congregational Church looks more hospitable and inviting since the railings have gone. Those railings bordering the footpath gave the impression that only those who kept to the straight and narrow path were welcome there! We hope that most of the old iron now going to the war factories has gone for ever. There were too many forbidding railings and fences in this country.

The war has shown that they were unnecessary. Well-behaved people will respect private property, even though it is unfenced. The ill-behaved are not made well-behaved merely by fences. Only the slow process of education and improving environments will do that.

August 6/43 It is a matter of some mystification, and not a little indignation, to many residents here that the removal of railings and gates has been effected with so little discrimination. Recently, houses facing a busy road have lost their gates, despite the fact that this endangers the lives of small children, while in some roads which are cul-de-sacs with very light traffic, gates, railings and chains have been left. And in most cases there are no children in the houses concerned. We should be interested to know who made the selection and on whose authority the exceptions were allowed where there are no children. Surely artistic value (if that constituted the grounds for exception) should be given second place. Where the removal of gates has put children in peril they should be replaced free of charge by another type of gate. Working people seldom own the house they live in, and cannot insist on the landlord doing this replacement.
Yours, etc., M. Tite, Deaconess, Westcott.

August 13/43 Iron railings: Another Grumble.
Sir:- In last weeks issue of "The Dorking Advertiser" was a letter referring to the seeming injustice in the selection of local gates and railings for iron scrap. Ratepayers know that the Government requires metal, but some would like to know why it is required from one house and not from another. For instance, why remove a small iron gate 3ft. wide from a house on the main road in which live five children under nine years of age, and leave large iron gates (which have not been closed for at least two years), and heavy railings in front of a house not now used as an ordinary residence? Why remove 12 yards of light spiked railings from a private house and leave 46 yards and two heavy gates of the same type on one side of woodland and 235 yards and two gates on the other side of the same woodland?

Why remove from one private house railings rusty to crumble when touched, and leave 7.5 yards of heavy ornamental chain outside another? To catalogue all the anomalies would take a column of your paper if this village were assessed.

It is not surprising if some inhabitants would be interested to learn what qualifications went to the surveying? Was the person responsible an expert in metal. Whoever did the job appeared to have little common sense.
Yours etc, E.R. Pringle, Wintershaw, Westcott.

Miss Pringle must have been feeling very sore when she wrote this letter as the railings were taken from Wintershaw.

August 30/43 This week we learn of another local award. A bar to the George Cross has been awarded to Lieut. Michael Arthur

Clinton, G.C., R.E., for conspicuous gallantry in carrying out hazardous work in a very brave manner. He received the George Cross in February 1942 for similar gallantry.

December 3/43   A fine piece of voluntary war work is now in full swing in Dorking. Go to the old chapel just off Church Street any morning or afternoon, from Monday to Friday, and you will see there a party of people busy threading lengths of narrow material, dark brown, green or sand coloured between the interstices of nets stretched over wooden frames. This work is called furbishing camouflage nets. Everyone has seen the camouflage nets covering Army vehicles. They are used in almost all theatres of war. They are used by the Navy and the R.A.F. as well as considerably, by the Army. They save lives and equipment. The call for them is incessant.

The nets, plain and unfurbished, are maunfactured by makers of fishermen's nets. The W.V.S. and other volunteers have been asked to undertake the job of converting the plain nets into camouflage nets. The Dorking W.V.S. ever ready to help in the war effort, has organised the local share of this big job for nimble fingers. The work is quite pleasant, too, because the workers can chat as they work.

The Dorking W.V.S. have found an admirable place for this work. Despite an unprepossessing exterior, the main part of the old chapel is a clean, bright and cheerful hall. There is a fire to warm it, and of course, that fire is used to boil the kettle for the inevitable cup of tea. The work goes on daily from 10 a.m. to 1 p.m., and from 2 to 5 p.m., from Mondays to Fridays, and there is an evening session on Wednesdays, from 5 to 9 p.m. Most of the workers are women, but there are also a few men workers, and more of both sexes will be welcome, for there is a lot of work to be done. One of the furbishers, a Westcott lady, is aged 81. All who can spare time are urged to become net furbishers.

*   *   *

January 7/44   Four houses destroyed. Nine persons killed in air raid.

During the enemy air raid in the early hours of Wednesday morning, a bomb fell on the edge of the populated part of a Home Counties village (Watson Road, Westcott). The explosion reduced four houses to a heap of rubble, and damaged other houses in the vicinity. Nine persons were killed and several injured. Those killed were a man, two women, three boys, a girl and two babies.

The demolished houses stood at the end of a long street lined with houses each side. Beyond the demolished houses are open fields so that, had the bomb fallen twenty yards or so to the west or north, little damage would have been done. At least, there would not have been so many fatal casualties.

The rescue party and other Civil Defence workers laboured nobly to release all the victims from the wreckage in less than four hours after the fall of the bomb. Neighbours, too, were very kind in helping the injured, sheltering the homeless, and in providing cups of tea and other refreshment for the hard-worked Civil Defence parties.

One of the houses destroyed was the home of Mr. P.G. Wakeford. He was in a neighbouring town fire watching at a local authority's offices. He was called home to the news that his wife and two of his daughters, Barbara and Ann, had been killed. Another daughter, Mildred, had a remarkable escape. It has been her custom to go to a friend's house when raids commence. This time, she had just opened the front door when the bomb fell. She was injured, but not seriously. Mr. Wakeford's eldest daughter is serving in the A.T.S.

The youngest of the children killed was a girl aged two years. Oldest among the casualties was a woman aged 92, who was injured.

Two boys, who were evacuees from London, were killed in one of the houses. They were in bed together in a ground floor room when the bomb fell. The force of the explosion turned their bed upside down, and the floor of the room immediately above collapsed on top of the bed. Their bodies were taken from beneath the bed.

Houses nearby were much damaged. The one immediately next door was the home of the Worsfold family. John Worsfold, a soldier serving in the R.E.M.E., arrived home on Tuesday evening on sick leave from North Africa. On Wednesday, while he was helping his relatives to salvage their belongings, he said to a reporter:"I did not bother about the raid until I heard a plane diving and a bomb coming. I thought it was going to hit us so I rolled under the bed and I was not hurt." His mother and his sister were injured.

Canadian soldiers joined in the salvage work throughout Wednesday. This was the biggest single tragedy that has ever fallen on the village. The names of those killed are as follows: Nellie Ada Wakeford, Barbara Wakeford, Ann Catherine Shirley Wakeford, John Henry Berg, Frederick Williams, Clara Ann Gravett, Anne Heather Robinson, Michael John Robinson and Alfred Lillywhite.

The Chairman of the Urban District Council visited the village on Friday afternoon in company with the Vicar, talking to some of those injured or bereaved by the bomb, and thanking neighbours who helped the injured, gave temporary homes to the homeless, and distributed refreshments to the men of the rescue parties searching among the debris for victims.

Relief fund opened. The Government departments concerned, and the local authorities, are taking every possible care to save those who suffered through the raid from enduring further anxiety through lacking the necessities of life. Members of an

85

F/O Richard Raspin inspecting the wreckage in Parsonage Lane, Westcott.

See page 87

Assistance Board have been meeting each morning in a house where accommodation has been provided by Miss Pringle, and they have been distributing money and clothing coupons to the persons affected by the raid requiring such help. Members of the local W.V.S. have been issuing clothing from the stock they held to meet such an emergency as this. But, above that official aid, local residents know that further aid would be useful to the sufferers in this time of need. Therefore, a Raid Relief Fund has been opened, and already £110 has been subscribed. A company of local residents met on Tuesday evening to elect a committee to administer the fund. The squire of the village was elected to the chair, and a committee of ten was appointed to organise a house-to-house collection throughout the village and to administer the fund.

March 3/44 German bomber crashes.
A village in the home counties (Westcott) which has previously sustained loss of life and property through enemy action had the satisfaction of being the graveyard of a German bomber which crashed during one of the air raids last week. The plane, a Dornier, came spinning down, out of control, struck a tree and landed in a well populated district of the village, with one of its wings touching the wall of a house. That it did not land on any house was fortunate, and still more fortunately the bombs it was carrying did not explode.

The plane had a crew of four, two of these baled out and landed in a village about two miles from where their plane crashed, and after firing pistol lights to attract attention to themselves, were captured by a special constable living nearby, and taken to a well known inn in the locality (Wotton Hatch Hotel). The other two members of the plane's crew were found dead with their plane. Many people in the village and surrounding districts saw the bomber spinning to its doom. It was showing its navigation lights.

Bomb disposal squad and R.A.F. men rendered the bombs harmless and dismantled the bomber. Some of the houses near the plane were temporarily evacuated.

The navigator of the British night fighter which shot the bomber down, visited the village on Sunday to see his victim. He apologised to the residents in the neighbourhood for having caused the Dornier to fall so close to their houses.

My own findings of this incident are as follows:

The German bomber crash at Westcott, February 24th 1944. Many stories have been told by local people concerning this crash; many are pure fiction. This account is the correct one, as told by both English and German crew members.

The story starts at Eindhoven in Holland on the night of February 24th 1944. The German unit was the 3rd Squadron/Bomber Wing 2 (III/K.G.2.) and the unit badge was the Holzhammer. The

On the left — Leut. Walter Kuttler, pilot of the Dornier who was killed in the crash.
See page 89

Julius Schurgers and Georg Trunsperger receive the Iron Cross from the Squadron Leader.
See page 89

plane, a Dornier 217-M which had a crew of four, these were: Lt. Walter Kuttler, pilot, aged 23 years. Sergeant and Air Gunner, Erwin Brieger, aged 22 years. Corporal and Observer, Georg Trunsperger, aged 21 years. Corporal and Air Gunner, Julius Schurgers aged 22 years.

Take off was at 8.30 pm, course about 300 degrees, height 15-20000 feet, Target, "King George V" Docks. Caught in a searchlight and a night fighter shot part of the tail unit away, got into a spin - time to bale out but couldn't owing to the centrifugal force. "Only the altimeter showed us how many feet we yet had for living" said a crew member.

Two were able to bale out and two went down with the plane. Landed in a parklike ground (The Vale of Wotton). These two were Georg Trunsperger and Julius Schurgers. They were taken to Wotton Hatch Hotel. Georg Trunsperger broke his foot and was taken to Dorking Hospital and Julius Schurgers to London for interrogation and then to Scotland for three months; then he was shipped to America, New York, New Jersey, Alabama, South and North Carolina, Georgia and Florida; this was for three and a half years. Repatriated to Germany in September 1947, his own home was bombed out.

The pilot, Walter Kuttler was found dead in the wreckage and Erwin Brieger was found behind a shed in Parsonage lane with his parachute half open. They were buried in Dorking Cemetery and in 1962 their remains were removed to Cannock Chase. This is a German Military cemetery.

The R.A.F. report gives seven unexploded bombs, 3 x 1100 lb. High explosive and 4 x 110 lb. incendiary bombs.

The English version of the crash is: The Dornier was shot down by a Mosquito of No.29 Night Fighter Squadron. A flight from this squadron was based at the naval aerodrome at Ford in Sussex to give added cover to the Portsmouth area during the build up to D-day. Several Mosquitos were ordered off from Ford about 9.00 p.m. Searchlights lit up the German. The pilot of the Mosquito was Sdn/Ldr.Clive Kirkland and his Navigator F/O Richard Raspin. "I believe Clive fired two bursts of cannon fire, hitting the "217" in the starboard engine - and the plane went into a dive, pieces were flying off its wing". Richard Raspin was taken the following day to the crash site. "We were not told about the German aircrew - or any other details. On the 25th we were patrolling as usual".

The squadron report is: 29 Squadron R.A.F.-Ford, 24 Feb.1944. Mosquito, 167. S/Ldr.C.Kirkland. F/O.R.C.Raspin. Up 21.31. Down 23.10. Scrambled to searchlights. 1 DO 217 destroyed.

<u>March 17/44</u> German plane crashes in flames.
A German twin-engine plane crashed in flames in a wood near a Home Counties town (Near Blackbrook, Holmwood Common) during the raid on Tuesday night. It caused no damage excepting by smashing

89

the trees among which it fell, and the only casualties were among the plane's crew. Almost certainly, the plane was brought down by a British fighter. Cannon fire was heard immediately before the plane fell in flames. Soon after it hit the ground, there was an explosion of petrol, and the wreckage was burnt out. All the crew were killed.

For the aircraft enthusiast I record a copy of the R.A.F. report on this crash:

Report Serial No.228 dated 18 March 1944. Report 8/69 - Ju 88 A-4. On the night of the 14/15 March 6 enemy aircraft crashed on land, with one exception they were all completely destroyed and very little information could be obtained from the site examination.

This aircraft was shot down by a night fighter and crashed at 23.05 hours on 14 March at Blackbrook, Holmwood Common, Nr. Dorking, Surrey. The aircraft was on fire in the air and dived almost vertically in the ground, the wreckage being entirely destroyed by fire and impact.

Identification Marking: None obtained.

The camouflage of the upper surfaces was a light blue grey mottled with dark green. The under surfaces were spray painted black, whilst the engine cowlings were yellow with wavy lines of black.

Crew: Three accounted for dead in wreckage.

In September 1972 Parts of a German fighter - bomber, a Junkers Ju 88 were uncovered on Holmwood Common on Tuesday, under the supervision of an official of the Battle of Britain Museum and the National Trust warden.

Mr. R. Mills from the museum said the main parts found on the common were one of the two engines, a whole wheel assembly including a tyre and undercarriage unit, and a turbo-charger. There were also numerous pieces of broken metal and other articles, including first aid kits, compressed air bottles, a pair of scissors - and a burnt piece of parachute.

Mr. Mills explained that an R.A.F recovery team would have come to the spot after the crash and, as well as collecting prisoners or dead bodies, would have salvaged most of the plane.

When all the parts of the plane had been salvaged and examined, the hole - which was about 8ft. to 10ft. deep in parts - was filled in and the ground was levelled off.

April 22/1944 Part of Vincent Lane was machine gunned by a lone German.
[From A.R.P. map].

<u>April 28/44</u> Many people have been stopping in front of one of the big windows at Messrs. Burton's premises in High Street, Dorking to study an interesting and neatly conceived propaganda display. Telling the story "Save water to save fuel" the display has been arranged by the Dorking Water Co. with Messrs. Burton's co-operation. There is a bath with a five inches "Plimsoll" line like the King's bath. There is a continuously running tap and a dripping cistern, and a water pipe wrapped with asbestos, newspapers and sacking to stress that pipes should be protected against the frost so as to avoid bursts which waste fuel. By the way, we are not offended by seeing in the display that a copy of the "Dorking Advertiser" has been used to wrap a pipe. The "Dorking Advertiser" is, we venture to suggest, so warmly sympathetic to good causes that is must be just the right texture to defeat hard, uncharitable frost.

There is one deliberate untruth in the display. A tap, suspended on a piece of string, is left running to waste, apparently, a continuous flow of water, and the public are told by a printed notice, "Four tons of coal a year are required to keep a cold water tap running at this rate. But this water is not wasted. It runs back to the water works along another piece of string". After long research, we have discovered that the water does not flow back along a piece of string. Into the nozzle of the tap is fitted a glass tube, the other end of which connects with a quarter-h.p. electric motor. The motor pumps water up the glass tube from a bowl hidden below the visible washing basin, and the water overflows down the outside of the tube, giving the illusion of a solid jet of water. In gratitude to Messrs. Burtons for their co-operation in making this display, the Dorking Water Co. have handed to them £5.5s to be given to the Dorking Youth Centre, which is accommodated above Messrs. Burton's shop.

I remember this display well, all the children and a number of adults thought it was the wonder of the age. (D.K.).

<u>May/June/44</u> Preparation for "Overlord".

In the Spring of 1944, one lane of the A24 dual carriageway between Dorking and Leatherhead unobtrusively filled up with a long line of parked military vehicles under camouflage netting. No one said a word. In June they disappeared as quietly as they had come. It was D-day. (E.O.M.).

<u>June 9/44</u> Westcott. Boys as maids and gardeners. To support the volunteer teams from the Scout movement under the scheme arranged by the Council of British Societies for Relief Abroad, May 20th was set aside as the day when every Cub and Scout was to earn at least a shilling towards the cost of equipping and maintaining Scout teams in the field. In Westcott, the 17th Dorking (Westcott) Pack of Cubs and Troop of Scouts went to it with a will. The houses in the area were circulated asking if the occupiers would provide a job of work for the boys, and when the replies came in they sorted and allocated to the boys

according to their capabilities. Starting early in the morning and working until late evening, a wide variety of jobs were done - weeding gardens and paths, stacking logs, cleaning windows, to household chores, the latter causing one small scout to exclaim that he had caught "house-maid's knee". Realising the great need by the peoples of the occupied and devastated countries for this scheme, the employers of this young but enthusiastic band of amateur housemaids and gardeners supported it magnificently, and instead of the shilling per head asked for by headquarters, the boys earned approximately 9s. per head, and were able to pay into the fund a grand total of £13.10s.(I was one of these small boys and earned 3s.6d.)

June 23/44 Leading Fireman Cyril Hills of the National Fire Service at Dorking, has been commended in orders issued by the Fire Force Commander of No.32 area for promptness and showing initiative at a fire caused by enemy action in February last (23rd). The call was to a fire at a farm (Woolcock Farm near Stonebridge, Dorking). Arriving there in charge of a fire pump crew, Hills saw that three haystacks had been set alight. Seeing that the third of the stacks was near a big barn and that the barn was in danger, he first gave orders that a line of hose should be run from a nearby pond to stop the fire spreading to the barn. Then while he was hurrying forward the work of getting cows from cowstalls which were threatened by the burning stacks, a man came to him saying: "Come to the farmhouse quickly. There is a bomb in the roof". Several men stood around the farmhouse. Smoke was coming from the roof. Hills was told he would be suffocated with smoke if he entered the house. Undismayed, he went in. He had to crawl on hands and knees because of the thick smoke. He climbed the stairs and along a couple of corridors into a bedroom where through clouds of smoke, he found the bomb. It had come through the roof and the bedroom ceiling, and had burnt through the floor boards until it rested on a 9 by 9 beam. Picking up a tin and a washstand mirror to protect him in case the bomb was of the explosive type. Hills crawled forward. Crawling back to the door he called for a bucket of water. This was brought to him. Crawling forward again, he threw the water over the bomb and it stopped burning immediately. Then Hills picked up the remains of the bomb and threw them out of a window. Through open windows and doors the smoke dispersed, and then, with saw and chisel, Hills cut away burning floorboards to complete the job of extinguishing the fire. His plucky perseverance and determination stopped a big fire. Hills has completed 17 years service as a fireman. He was a member of the Dorking Fire Brigade in peace time.

Flying bombs. The first flying bomb to drop on England was on June 13th 1944. They were launched from Northern France. The bombs are small jet-propelled aircraft carrying a ton of explosive in the nose and fitted with an automatic pilot. They fly at about 350 m.p.h, and after 150 miles a clockwork mechanism sends them into a dive to the ground.

The first of these flying bombs to this district fell in Norbury Park on Sunday June 18th.

<u>June 30/44</u>   Isolated cottage hit.

A flying bomb exploded one night this week (Monday June 26th)
within a few yards of an isolated cottage in Southern England,
the only house amid acres of open country. (Elm Cottage, Sandy
Lane, Dorking, now Milton Court Lane). The bomb exploded when it
crashed into trees near the cottage. Had its flight not been
stopped by the trees it would have fallen in fields and done no
great harm. As it was, the explosion demolished the cottage
standing completely isolated far from any military objective or
any built-up area. Three persons were killed - two women and a
boy. They were: Lilian Rose Lawrence, Royston Arthur Lawrence
and Irene Kathleen Risley.

<u>July 2/44</u>   A flying bomb fell near Headley Rectory. The bomb
fell about 20 yards from the Rectory.   In 1947 the house was
rebuilt. The garden was devastated. The walls remained standing
with the exception of the lean-to kitchen. The interior was
wrecked and the house made uninhabitable. All the out-buildings
and the gardener's cottage were badly damaged. The orchard was
badly damaged with the trees uprooted.

The Rector and his wife had heard the bomb approaching and just
had time to reach the shelter in the kitchen before the wall and
roof collapsed, they were not injured. Their furniture was badly
damaged and was removed to King's barn by local wardens and
Canadian soldiers.

The blast broke many windows, even as far away as Walton-on-
the-Hill.

Windows in the Rectory had previously been broken by a bomb
which fell in the wood a few hundred yards away on June 17th
1944. See: Headley Church records and Headley W.I. book 1962-65.

<u>July 7/44</u> Flying bombs fall in fields and woods. Illustrating
how indiscriminate is the aiming of the flying bombs, many have
fallen in fields and woods in Southern England, where they have
merely damaged or blown down some trees.   In one extensive police
division covering two towns and numerous big and small villages,
only one of the bombs has caused fatal injuries. (Elm Cottage).
In one other an elderly lady died through heart failure, due to
shock, when a bomb fell a few hundred yards from her cottage.
(This was Elizabeth Cheeseman aged 74 years who lived at
St. Albyn's Cottages, Ockley; this bomb fell on June 30th).
Blast from bombs has broken windows and torn off doors and tiles,
but in no case has serious damage been done to property of
national importance.

<u>July 14/44</u> Tackling Bombs - Phosphorus bombs may be among the
enemy's air missiles. Controlling these fire-raising bombs
demands a technique different from that used against other
incendiaries. It is a technique not over difficult to master.
But if the correct methods are not known and a person tries to

Flying bomb damage at Headley Rectory.

See page 93

tackle a Phosphorus bomb without taking the essential precautions, he or she risks being seriously, even mortally harmed. The best way of learning the phosphorous bomb technique is by practical demonstration. Recently Mr. J.C. Funnell (Fire Guard Officer for Dorking) and his assistants, have been giving such demonstrations to wardens, fire guards and others. The most recent of these was on last Friday evening at Milton Court, where the spectators included Westcott wardens and fire guards and men of the National Fire Service. Messrs. Funnell, Petts and one other, working admirably showed the ways of getting the burning phosphorus under control in various circumstances and of dealing with the incipient fires caused by splashes from the bombs. It was an interesting demonstration, made memorable by Mr. Funnell's concise commentary enlivened with touches of humour. A similar demonstration will be given on July 25, beginning at 3 p.m. near the Pippbrook Mill House, London Road. This demonstration is being staged chiefly for the instruction of Southern Railway workers, but members of the general public and particularly fire guards will be welcome. Lessons which may be valuable will be learnt there.

<u>August 4/44</u> Bomb destroys Church. A flying bomb fell on a country church in Southern England (Abinger) just before morning service was due to begin yesterday morning. As the bomb was falling the Rector was on his way to church. He was not injured. Rescue men, firemen and soldiers searched the rubble in case people had got to church early for the service, but no one was found.

The nave of the church was early Norman. Almost all the building, including the wooden belfry and the oak shingled spire were destroyed. Only the eastern end stands.

Blast from the bomb also damaged an ancient manor house and a well-known inn nearby. Many of the church yard tombstones were smashed.

<u>September 15/44</u> Abinger Church destroyed by flying bomb. Early Norman craftmanship, now in ruins.

It can now be disclosed that the beautiful old Parish Church of St. James at Abinger was, to a large extent, demolished by a flying bomb on a Thursday in August.(3rd). The West end of the Church was completely destroyed. The East end and parts of the North and South walls are still standing, but the walls are much cracked, and it is possible they will have to be pulled down before the Church is rebuilt.

The bomb fell a few minutes before the 8 o'clock service was due to begin. Fortunately, no one was in the Church at the time and there were no casualties. The Rector, Rev. L.G. Meade, was just leaving the Rectory to walk across to the Church. In fact, when the explosion occurred, he was at the front door of the Rectory. It happened that morning that he was a few seconds later than usual in starting for the Church.

Abinger Church destroyed by a Flying bomb.

See page 95

The Domesday Survey of 1086 records the existence of a Church at Abinger. Although some good architects, among them the late Sir Gilbert Scott and Mr. Philip Johnson (an expert on Surrey Churches), have expressed their belief that part of Abinger Church was Saxon, the more generally held opinion is that the North and South walls of the nave were early Norman. These walls, built of rubble, were nearly four feet thick up to the windows. Of the six small round-headed Norman windows, three on each side high up in the nave, only one is left in the part of the walls still standing. This one is on the south side, and here also remains a lovely 15th century three light window. However, it is probable that these walls, broken and cracked, will have to be demolished when the Church is rebuilt. Possibly then the ancient windows may be re-incorporated in the new walls.

Next in antiquarian importance after the early Norman nave was the North aisle alongside the chancel. Its rubble-built walls and its seven lancet windows were, according to some authorities, built as early as 1200, while no authority has put them as later than 1240. This aisle is commonly called the Patron's Chancel, since the patron claimed it to be his private property, as in the case of similar chapels in many other Churches. The patrons have been, for many centuries, the Evelyns, squires of Wotton. The present patron is Mr. C.J.A. Evelyn, a descendant of John Evelyn, the Diarist.

None of the walls of this North aisle have fallen in the bomb destruction of the Church, but all the walls have been severely cracked, and it is not certain they can be kept in position when rebuilding takes place.

The roof, the belfry and spire, the South doorway and porch are all gone. They are now a distressing heap of rubble amidst blasted trees and broken tombstones. The doorway and porch were made in 1857 in the 13th century style, the porch being given by local farmers to replace a much smaller brick porch. The great tie beams in the roof, the kingposts, rafters and ceiling boards were 600 or more years old. That grand, long-enduring workmanship by the old craftsmen is now splintered into firewood and debris.

In the belfry were three bells. All have been recovered from among the debris although, possibly, they have been cracked by the explosion and will need recasting. Two are inscribed "William Eldridge made mee, 1674".

Most of the Church plate and the old parish registers (beginning in 1559) were in a bank safe on that fateful August morning, and thus have been preserved. And the current registers were in a safe in the vestry at the east end of the Church. They were not damaged.

Most of the mural monuments and all the brasses from the Church have been recovered intact. But one marble mural monument from

the west side of the main south door has gone. Few of the
tombstones in the immediate vicinity of the Church escaped
damage. All the upright stones on the south side were torn up or
broken into two or more pieces. The lofty Cross of the memorial
erected to the memory of the Abinger men and women who died in
the 1914-18 War was blown off its pedestal, and it broke into
three pieces. This memorial was designed by Sir Edwin Lutyens.

F/O Richard Raspin navigator and Sqdn./Ldr. Clive Kirkland pilot. The crew of the
Mosquito who shot down the German. *See page 89*

The Church crypt was undamaged. In the days of the 1940 and 1941 air raids, the crypt was the school children's shelter. It has now been proved that it was a safe place.

The bomb which destroyed the Church damaged also other interesting old buildings nearby, notably the Manor House and the Abinger Hatch inn, Abinger Common Schools, the Rectory, and other houses also suffered window and ceiling damage. Since their return from Italy at the beginning of the war, Sir Max and Lady Beerbohm have been living in the Manor House Cottage, a hundred yards from the Church. This place was so badly damaged by the bomb that Sir Max and Lady Beerbohm had to evacuate to a friend's house nearby.

Since the destruction of the Church, services have been held wherever possible - in the schools (despite smashed windows), in a N.A.A.F.I. canteen, in the dining room at the Hatch inn. It is possible that the Church will find a semi-pernament home in the Institute next to the Hatch inn. The schools were re-opened to the children on August 14th.

A fund has been opened for the eventual re-building of the Church and for the setting up, in the meantime, of a place where services can be held until the new Church arises.

<u>August 22/48</u> Bombed Church Rises Again. Rebuilding begins at Abinger.

Four years, almost to the day, after its destruction by a flying bomb, the work of rebuilding Abinger Parish Church has begun.

For some time services were held wherever possible - in the nearby school, a N.A.A.F.I. canteen, and in Goddards (a private house). When temporary work was carried out to preserve the remains of the building until reconstruction could begin, the least damaged part of the Church, the North aisle, was roofed and boarded of from the chancel and nave. In the small but pleasant chapel so formed the spiritual life of the parish has been centred, while, as a reminder of the work still to be done, the worshippers have had a view, through a window in the temporary wall, of wild flowers growing on the ruined South wall of the nave.

Breeze blocks were used to fill in the arches and to help support the remaining part of the roof, above the altar. Bomb-blast stripped the roof timbers, and the lychgate, of their Horsham stone tiles, and a covering of weatherproofed felt temporarily replaced them, completing the "first aid" rendered until the necessary licence and permission to begin rebuilding could be obtained. It was believed that the bomb exploded in the air after hitting the belfry, its spire, or possibly a tall cypress tree which grew close to the South-West corner of the nave. The West and South walls suffered the most damage; the West wall of the nave, including the belfry, spire and the great tie-beam which supported them, being completely demolished. Also demolished were the South door and porch, a great part of the North wall and the South wall, up to a point beyond the porch. The North and South walls were the most ancient part of the Church. The remains of the bomb fell in the paddock outside the West wall of the Churchyard and they have been collected and stacked neatly under a hawthorn tree on the bank by the footpath which runs from the Churchyard to Abinger Manor, also damaged by the blast.

At last a licence was granted for reconstruction work to be undertaken as far as the eaves and at the beginning of this month work was commenced by the well known firm of building contractors, Messrs. Trollope and Colls, Ltd. They are working under the direction of the architect, Mr. F. Etchells, who has planned to reconstruct the Church as an almost exact replica of the one destroyed. His original plans, not finally approved in detail, provide, however, for some small but interesting deviations, which will have the effect of restoring the Southern aspect of the Church to something like it was before 1879 and the interior appearance will be changed - if the plans are approved - by the installation of the organ and choir at the back, or West, end of the Church instead of, as formerly, in front of the congregation, on either side of the chancel. In this connection it is interesting to recall that until 1856, when it was removed, there was a large Singers' Gallery across the West end, in which there were "a bass-viol, clarionet, etc. for the band". The changes will involve dispensing with the badly damaged South aisle, which contained the old vestry and the organ, also considerably damaged and now exposed to the weather.

The debris was cleared up four years ago by a party of forty Italian Pioneers, former prisoners of war, under the direction of the Rector and a British Army Officer. They collected into dumps great quantities of fallen timber, stone roof slabs and broken gravestones and later salvaging and clearing work added to these dumps. The builders are using as much of the material from the old Church as possible in the new building, and any more that is needed will be obtained from Leith Hill - the old Church having been constructed of Leith Hill stone. As the present licence covers only the erection to eave level no decision on the roofing materials has yet been taken. So far the foundations have been dug at the West end of the Church and filled in with concrete, about six feet wide, to take the new walls, which like the old "early Norman" walls whose remains still stand, will be nearly four feet thick.

Great oak beams, given by the Hon. Mrs. Vaughan, and cut on her estate at High Ashes, Abinger, are already on the site and the three bells recovered from the debris are intact and will be rehung. In the new Church they will not, however, be tolled by bell ringers, a hand chime arrangement being planned. Part of the cost of rebuilding will be met from the building fund opened soon after the destruction of the Church and contributed to by parishioners and the many tourists whose curiosity is aroused by the ruin and who invariably express their dismay that in all the square miles of open country the well-loved and beautiful little Parish Church should feel the full force of the Nazi penchant for indiscriminate destruction. Grants towards the rebuilding have been made also by the Bishop of Guildford's Challenge Fund and the War Damage Commission, whose architects originally reported the Church as "a total loss".

September 15/44 Flying bomb victims thanks. Sir:- In these days, when so often the Government and Rural Council's departments are criticised for red tape and delay, I think it is only fair to acknowledge publicly the promptitude shown by the Dorking and Horley Rural District Council in sending their Surveyor to examine the damage caused by flying bombs in this part of Surrey. Some time ago a bomb fell on the outskirts of this village, causing a good deal of damage to two cottages and my house. It happened at 2 a.m., and besides the kindness shown and assistance given to us by our wardens, at 9 a.m. the Surveyor was on the spot with our local builder. There and then immediate repairs were decided upon, and work was started at once. Our roof was repaired that very day. In the course of four days our windows with plate glass were all in (there were many of them and all large ones).

A second flying bomb which fell on our Village Green after 8 o'clock one evening caused much damage to some cottages and buildings nearby. On this occasion, too, the repairs were started immediately the next morning. Our builder with his own workmen and those of neighbouring villages, forming a pool gang, did marvels. Almost every tile on the roof of the Village Hall was off, and all the windows smashed, yet by the evening the roof was in proper order quite repaired and all windows neatly blocked, and the hall, which is used for a Y.M.C.A. canteen and Rest Centre, was fit to be used again. The men worked all Saturday and Sunday carrying out urgent repairs to various premises.

This was done with a good will and cheerfulness which deserve our praise and gratitude.
Yours etc. Adine O'Neill, Southfield Ockley.

September 29/44 20 flying bombs fell in the Dorking Urban District. If any of the flying bombs were aimed at Dorking - which, of course, was not the case: it was a haphazard form of attack - not a single bullseye was scored. The town escaped marvellously. The nearest to scoring "inners" were the bombs which fell at Pixham, in the chalkpit near Dorking Town Station and at Flint Hill.

It may now be revealed that twenty flying bombs fell in the Dorking Urban District. Three which fell outside the boundary also caused damage in the Urban District. The full casualty list was three persons killed, one seriously injured (since recovered), and 28 slightly injured.

On one day in July five bombs fell: - (21st) At Mickleham; Old School Lane, Brockham; Pixham; Flint Hill, North Holmwood; and in the chalkpit North of Dorking Town Station.

In August the Isolation Hospital at Westcott was seriously damaged by a bomb which fell in a field about 100 yards from the hospital buildings. None of the patients or staff was seriously hurt. They were transferred temporarily to Cuddington Isolation Hospital. The diphtheria block was damaged beyond repair. This block is being demolished, but the remainder of the buildings are being restored. The use of the scarlet fever wards was resumed at the beginning of September.

The first of the flying bomb visitors to this district fell in Norbury Park in June. The last was in August in the woods at the back of the swimming pool on Box Hill.

Many houses were damaged, some seriously, a lot slightly. In every case where the occupation of the house could be continued, first aid repairs were made promptly. Permanent repairs are being made as quickly as the state of the labour market permits.

A woman with three children who had evacuated from their London home when it was damaged by a flying bomb figured in two of the local bomb incidents. She moved from London to Brockham. She was bombed out from there and, because the children were slightly affected by a skin disease, the mother and the children were given accommodation in a hut at the Isolation Hospital. Here again, on August 4th, this family's temporary home was made uninhabitable. Still the woman remained wonderfully perky. She merely remarked "God is with us".

All these flying bomb incidents, coming in the space of a few weeks, severely tested the Civil Defence services. Everyone agrees that the services came through the test magnificently. There was not a second's avoidable delay, there was assistance for the sufferers, and there was a full measure of kindly sympathy supported by practical help of the right sort. All sections of the Civil Defence (and in this the Police must be included) did their jobs magnificently. To all, from the Sub-Controller downwards, the thanks of the community are due. The rescue parties had some tough jobs. They did them well. The public assistance officials forgot officialdom, giving help regarding food, clothes, etc, immediately without the inquisition normally associated with public assistance.

A neat technique was introduced to get help where needed quickly. When the alert was given, a spotter went to the high roof at Pippbrook, his station there being connected by telephone to the Report Centre. When the spotter saw a bomb fall, he reported the approximate district to the Report Centre. A rescue party lorry, an ambulance, a car for sitting cases, and the A.R.P. officer, or his deputy, set off immediately to the named district and, if necessary, they called at the warden's post there to get the exact location. Through this system, helpers were on the spot within a few minutes.

49 Flying bombs in rural district. Most fell in fields.

In the extensive Dorking and Horley Rural district, from Horley in the east to Abinger in the west, 49 flying bombs have fallen. The casualties were one woman, aged 74, killed at Ockley, and 50 persons injured.

Not a single parish in the whole area escaped. The numbers of bombs falling in the parishes were: - Abinger 5, Betchworth 5, Buckland 2, Charlwood 5, Capel 1, Headley 7, Holmwood 5, Horley 5, Leigh 1, Newdigate 6, Ockley 2, Wotton 5. Most of the bombs fell in fields and woods.

Since the beginning of the war to date, the total casualties in the rural district have been: Killed 6, injured and taken to hospital 36, slightly injured 101. The six fatal casualties were: A man aged 65 and a woman aged 60, killed at Horley; a woman aged 47, killed at Buckland; a man aged 47 and a woman aged 51, killed at Charlwood; and the only fatal flying bomb casualty, a woman aged 74, at Ockley.

In the flying bomb attacks, five houses were totally destroyed, eight were so damaged as to make demolition necessary. 32 were seriously damaged, and 992 slightly damaged. Prior to D-Day - that means prior to the flying bomb attacks - figures for house casualties were: Totally destroyed 7, so badly damaged as to need demolition 12, seriously damaged 42, slightly damaged 1,295.

In the Dorking and Horley Rural District, as elsewhere, the Civil Defence services gave efficient and sympathetic help to sufferers through flying bombs. A wide and sparsely populated rural district such as this has its own peculiar problems for Civil Defence services. The calls on transport and communications are more severe than in a compact district. Yet the rescue and ambulance services of public assistance and house repairers followed up quickly.

October 13/44 Dorking's Air Raid Experiences.

A large scale map of the Dorking Urban District is being prepared at Pippbrook by the A.R.P. officer, Mr. T.M. Ward, to show where enemy air raid bombs have fallen since the beginning of the war. The marks on the map are varied in colour and shape in order to indicate whether the bomb was a high explosive (exploded or unexploded), a flying bomb, a basket of incendiaries, and so on, and the date of the incident is placed against each mark. The map bears a lot of sinister looking marks. Some day, possibly soon, the map will be publicly exhibited.

The following is a record of the numbers of bombs, excluding flying bombs, which have fallen in the Dorking district:-

Dorking town: 77 high explosives, 10 oil incendiary bombs,

about 50 other incendiary bombs. Westcott: 50 high explosives, one para-bomb, 2 oil incendiaries, about 785 other incendiaries. Brockham: 52 high explosives, 7 oil incendiaries, about 600 other incendiaries, Mickleham and Westhumble: 42 high explosives, 2 oil incendiaries, about 300 other incendiaries. Box Hill: 44 high explosives, 2 oil incendiaries, about 100 other incendiaries. North Holmwood: 11 high explosives, 3 oil incendiaries, about 500 other incendiaries. Ranmore: 19 high explosives, about 400 incendiaries.

A study of the map reveals that Dorking residents had several providential escapes. Many of the map marks, are in long lines showing where sticks of bombs fell across the area without, in most cases, hitting buildings. In August, 1940, the enemy dropped a string of bombs stretching from Goodwyns Farm in a North-Westerly direction up to the railway line below Ranmore. There were in this string of bombs 14 high explosives, two of which did not explode.

Three months later, Dorking had a stick of nine bombs starting at the Vicarage at the foot of Vincent Lane, and going across the Water Company's meadows to the railway. On May 24th 1941, seven high explosives fell in the Pixham Lane area, mostly on railway land, but without damaging the railway lines. On May 11th 1941, nineteen high explosives fell in a long line among trees and bracken on Ranmore Common, well away from any houses.

Dorking's most narrow escape was on November 1st 1940, when a stick of bombs fell across the town from the Chart Lane corner of Marlborough Road to Vincent Lane sand pit. These bombs caused considerable damage to buildings, but no serious casualty. The last of the stick, a bomb which fell in the sand pit, did not explode.

The night of November 29th 1940, was an unpleasant night. A long string of bombs started at the "Barley Mow", Brockham (which was much damaged) and went on up to the top of Box Hill where the mansion of Brockham Warren was also hit. Another nasty night was that of October 29th 1940, when a bomb hit the corner of the Fraser Gardens housing estate, killing several people. The Fraser Gardens houses were built (largely through the encouragement of Sir Malcom Fraser, who gave the land) to rehouse people moved from cottages demolished under slum clearance schemes. By the way, it is strange that Council houses seem to have suffered more than private houses. There were sad examples of Council house damage at Marlborough Road and Fraser Gardens.

All but a few of the 2700 incendiary bombs fell in fields and woods. Only one big fire was caused by incendiary bombs. That was at Holmwood Park, an isolated country mansion, fired by incendiaries on October 29th 1940 - a few hours before a high explosive hit the Fraser Gardens houses.

Westcott's total of 785 incendiaries includes one big batch of 700 which fell in open country near Coast Hill, on March 25th

1941. Box Hill also had several big baskets of incendiaries. They did no important damage; they merely gave a sort of firework display on the hill slopes and made people stay out of doors to watch the display.

Prior to the coming of the flying bombs, seven houses in the Dorking urban area had been completely destroyed by air raid damage, three had been so seriously damaged that they had to be demolished, 51 houses were seriously damaged, and 694 were slightly damaged. The flying bomb attacks seriously damaged Elm Cottage so that it will have to be demolished, 13 other houses were seriously damaged, and about 650 have been slightly damaged.

October 13/44 Dorking residents remember the Divisional sign of the 11th British Armoured Division - a black bull on a yellow background "The charging bull" was the name Dorking gave to that sign when the Division was stationed for a few months in this district.

November 10/44 Dorking residents have been pleased this week to bid "Goodbye" - and good riddance to some of the concrete road blocks and big angle irons which littered the streets and made movement, particularly during the black-out, a risk to life and limb. The blocks which have gone so far are mostly the cylindrical things; the bigger blocks, which are a bigger obstruction, need a lot of pneumatic drilling to shift them. Another local improvement now beginning to be noticed is a faint illumination of the streets through the relaxation of the strictest black-out, allowing some light to come from windows overlooking the streets. On that subject of light, may we add a plea for better lighting in the subway at Dorking North Railway Station. That is a needlessly dark tunnel.

November 24/44 Au Revoir of No.7 Platoon Dorking's Home Guard.

No.7 Platoon "A" Company 7th Battalion, Surrey Home Guard, gathered at the Odd Fellows Hall Dorking on Thursday evening last week, for an "au revoir" dinner and concert. All the long hours of Guard duty, all the physical exertions and unaccustomed athletics undergone in training and drilling, even all the disappointments grousingly endured seem worthwhile now when farewells are being said. In standing down, the Home Guards appreciate the fun they have had amid strenuous battle training, and they appreciate all the new friendships they have formed.

November 24/44 The Dorking Home Guard will hold their farewell parade on Sunday, December 3rd. The various sections of Dorking's big "A" Company will march to the Meadowbank Recreation Ground for inspection by the inspecting officer, Lieut-Col. Lane, at 3 p.m. After a march past, the General Salute, the troops will march to the High Street where, at the wide part of the street with the two half Companies at either side the "Retreat" will be beaten and the final dismissal will be given by Col. Lane.

Dorking High Street with big angle irons which littered the streets.

See page 105

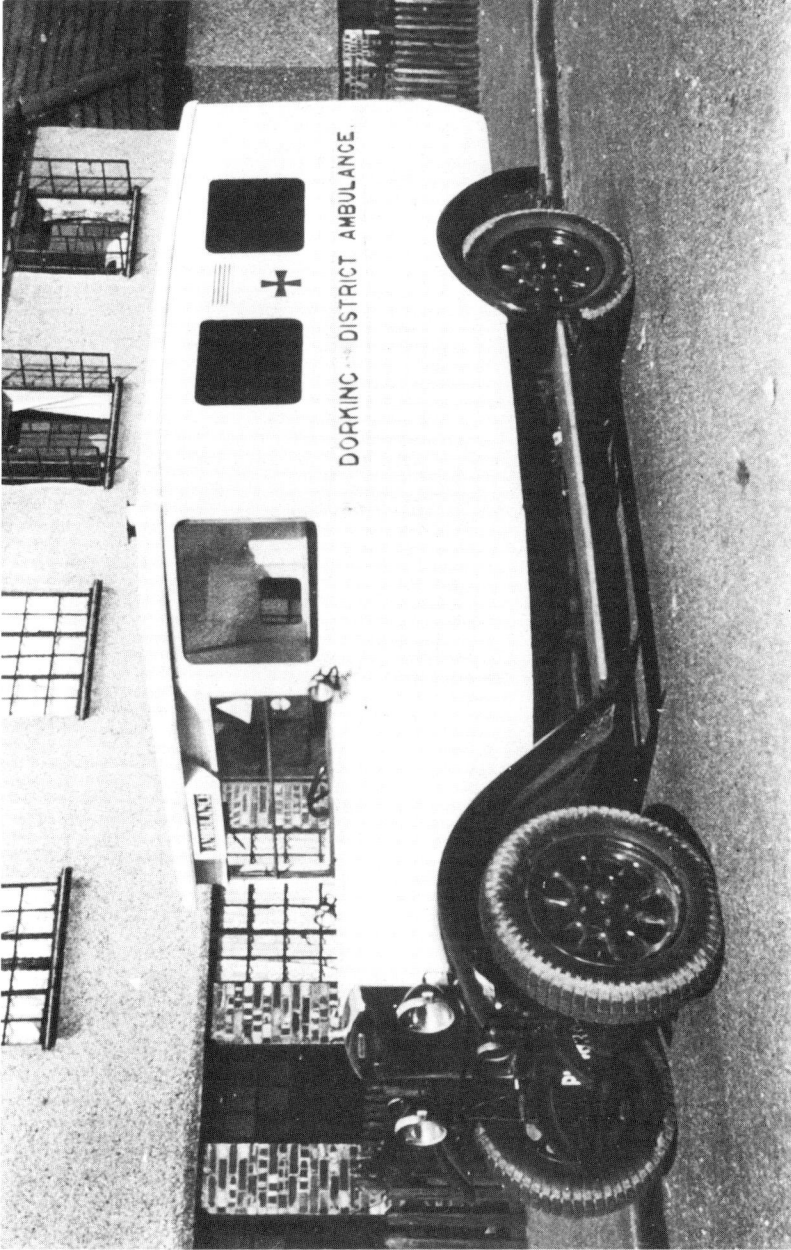

See page 109

Dorking's Morris ambulance.

107

No. 4 Platoon Dorking Home Guard.

See page 109

December 1/44 16 years hard Labour. Dorking Ambulance reaching its end. The Morris ambulance which was bought in January 1928, by public subscription from the Dorking townspeople has reached the end of its useful life - as an ambulance. The Urban District Council, given that news at their meeting last Tuesday, decided to invite tenders from anyone wishing to buy the ambulance, possibly for conversion into a caravan. The newer of the Dorking ambulances is, of course, still in service.

No one, said Major M. Chance, liked to part with an old friend, but the Morris ambulance was now no longer fit for ambulance work. Since it was bought on January 1st 1928, the ambulance had run 42,404 miles, it had been re-bored twice, and it had transported 2,274 patients. Before the Morris was bought, Dorking was served by an ambulance which was canvas covered and tremendously shaky. Those who subscribed to the purchase of the Morris ambulance would feel that their gifts had been well spent in providing a kindly service for sixteen years. Major Chance ended with the hope that as soon as the war was over, a fund would be raised to buy a new ambulance.

Both Major Chance and Mr. N.G. Wilkinson referred to the assistance given in the manning of the Dorking ambulances by members of the Civil Defence ambulance service. Since January 1st 1944, bearers from the Civil Defence Service had been supplied for the civil ambulance on 337 occasions, and, in addition, help had been given on 182 occasions in carrying civil cases in Civil Defence and County Council ambulances and on 162 occasions in carrying military cases in those ambulances. Mr. Wilkinson declared that no other region had such a devoted body of ambulance workers as had Dorking in its Civil Defence ambulance service, and Major Chance paid tribute to Mr. T.M. Ward (the A.R.P. officer), Mrs. Aarvold (the Ambulance Commandant), Mr. Knowles (Rescue party superintendent), and all members of their squads for the splendid work they had done to help the civil ambulance service.

December 8/44 Company - Dismiss. Dorking Home Guard break off from final parade.

With pride, relief and regret strangely mixed "A" (Dorking) Company of the 7th Battalion Surrey Home Guard paraded for the "stand down" last Sunday. It was an historic event. For four years these men have stood firm guarding Dorking until the risk of invasion passed and until the armies of liberation were ready for the decisive adventure of counter invasion.

The Dorking Home Guard are justifiably proud of having in their off-work time (one cannot call it leisure time) become a well-trained and disciplined company of soldiers. That pride was reflected in their martial bearing and smart alertness as they marched through Dorking streets for the final parade. There was, of course, relief that an invading army did not come, but there was also some regret that Home Guard drills and duty, which produced some fun and a lot of comradeship among all the

See page 109

No. 6 Platoon Dorking Home Guard.

inconveniences, have ended.

Memories of four years ago were revived by Sunday's Parade - memories of the somewhat haphazard beginnings of the Local Dorking Volunteers, memories of the weird assortment of arms and equipment hastily gathered together in those epic days, memories of uncomfortable nights made agreeable by comradeship.

Dorking saw last Sunday that her Home Guards have changed vastly (excepting in patriotism and comradeship) since the days of that first eager response to Mr.Eden's broadcast on the night of May 14th 1940. At their final parade, Dorking's Home Guard were well equipped, well armed; they had the smartness and steadiness of old soldiers, and one sensed the esprit de corps of a loyal body of men who were watching the Corps being disbanded. Five hundred men were on parade, for the Dorking Company is a big one of ten oversized platoons. At one time, with attached section, its roll was approaching a thousand. And it began as an enormous platoon of nearly 500.

Assembling at different points, the two half-companies and the Headquarters platoon marched separately to the Meadowbank Recreation Ground.

December 22/44 No. 8 Home Guard platoon "sits down".

December 29/44 No. 4 Platoon farewell.

            *   *   *

January 12/45 Almost all ten Platoons in "A" (Dorking) Company, 7th Battalion Surrey Home Guard, have now met for their farewell social gatherings.

February 9/45 Aeroplane crashes. Falls between two Capel Houses. An aeroplane crashed into the front garden of Mr. Willis's house in Vicarage Lane, Capel, on Wednesday. It fell ten yards from that house and 20 yards from the neighbouring house, but none of the occupants of the houses was hurt. All that happened apart from the smashing of the aeroplane was that big lumps of mud were thrown up by the impact, and some of these broke three windows and two tiles. One of the lumps hit a window near which a man aged 80 was shaving. It broke the window, but did not hurt the very much surprised shaver. The pilot of the plane, an American airman had left the aeroplane by parachute. He landed at Roll's Farm, Newdigate. In landing, one of his ankles was broken. He was taken to the Dorking and District Hospital.

This story continues with an extract from the West Sussex County Times. February 4th 1977.

Two groups of aviation enthusiasts are planning a dig for history in the village of Capel. They hope to recover the remains of a Mustang fighter plane which crashed in the area at the end of the Second World War.

The Surrey and Sussex Aviation Society and the Wealden Aviation Archaeological Group.

For the moment plans for the dig have been delayed as the clay in which the wreckage lies is too soft for excavation. It is hoped that the ground will have dried out enough to begin digging some time in March.

The plane probably belonged to the Royal Canadian Air Force. We are sure the pilot baled out before the crash.

May 27/1977 Bomber buffs told "no". Aircraft buffs are being banned from digging up the wreckage of a war-time bomber which crashed on Capel recreation ground.

Behind the ban are the Parish Council who own the field. They say the small amount of wreckage left does not warrant churning up their fields.

A Sussex aviation club had written first to Mole Valley Council about digging up the recreation ground. They were referred to the Parish Council. But at the last meeting councillors said that little wreckage remained.

Much of the plane, say the council, ended up in a private garden off the field. And most of that has been recovered.

February 16/45 Sergeant A. Rose and Sergeant C.W. Hughes, members of "A" (Dorking) Company, 7th Battalion, Surrey Home Guard have been honoured this week by the award by Lieut.- Gen. Sir Alan G. Cunninham, K.C.B, D.S.O, M.C.,(Commander in Chief Eastern Command) of "Certificates of Good Service" expressing appreciation of services rendered in the Home Guard and of devotion to duty. These certificates are equivalent to a mention in despatches - Sergeant Rose was "A" Company's assistant armourer.

February 16/45 Street lighting has returned to Dorking. But only with two lamps at present, and those two are only experimental - for this week only. One lamp giving a normal white light has been installed at Pump Corner and a blue one in High Street against the Post Office. The Pump Corner light is much brighter than the subdued war-time lighting we expected. It will help wheel and foot at that awkward corner. The blue light at the Post Office is, well, just a light sufficient to show where the kerb is. The two lights are being operated this week as an experiment. After this week the lights will be cut off until the Dorking Council decide what street lighting they will order within the limits of the dim-out restrictions. Most Dorking residents will welcome a return now of some form of general street lighting.

March 2/45 The part-time section of the National Fire Service is standing down - not disbanding in the same way as the Home Guard, but going "on the reserve", so that, no longer giving continuous nightly manning of the pumps, the firemen will be free from the normal rotas of duties, but will be available to be called for service in an emergency.

March 23/45 A Corporal of the Royal Highlanders of Canada was shot and killed during firing exercises at the Westcott rifle butts last week. A party of 16 men of a Canadian infantry training unit went to the range for rifle shooting instruction, 12 men were firing at the time. On the adjoining range, Bren guns were being fired. "Accidental death" was recorded; there was a possibility of a ricochet by a Bren gun bullet from the adjoining range.

(This was a very busy range, the noise echoed all through the valley).

April 20/45 Plane crashes on Dorking by-pass road. A R.A.F. reconnaissance plane (a Hudson) returning from a mission over Germany crashed on the Dorking by-pass road at a few minutes before 1 a.m. last Thursday morning. The crew of four baled out very shortly before the crash. They all landed in the vicinity, one reaching the ground less than a hundred yards from the plane. The pilot, the last man to leave, baled out only just in time.

Only one of the crew was hurt. In landing, he injured an ankle and had to be taken to hospital.

There was only one other minor casualty. Mr. Alfred Schermuly, who lives near the by-pass road, was one of the first to reach the crashed plane. Dressed only in pyjamas and a raincoat and with bare feet, he ran there, and fearing that members of the crew might be in the wreckage, he tried to pull parts of it away. In doing so he cut his right hand severely. However, he continued working energetically and helped the firemen when they arrived.

The main part of the plane fell on the concrete road and was smashed into a tangled mass of metal. The petrol caught fire. Immediately there was a big blaze. To make the crash more terrifying, exploding small arms ammunition kept up a crackling louder than the crackling of the fire. The flames were not extinguished until the firemen smothered the burning petrol with foam compound.

In falling, the plane passed close over the roof tops of houses in the Deepdene area. The noise awoke everyone, and from many bedroom windows people saw a tower of flames. They thought that the crash had set fire to the Deepdene mansion. Fortunately that was not so. The mansion escaped by about a hundred yards, and other houses around had providential escapes.

Mr. Frederick A. Elliott, 3 Cleardene, Dorking, writes: "In the aeroplane crash, the parachute landing of the pilot in close

113

A group of Dorking's Civil Defence volunteers.

See page 115

proximity to his burning aircraft makes it appear that he deliberately risked his life in order that the plane would clear the houses in the neighbourhood. I am sure townspeople will join with me in extending our heartfelt gratitude to the pilot for his heroic action. May he speedily recover from his injured ankle. If it is possible to obtain his name and address, I should like to write him personally, and I hope that the Council will officially recognise the bravery of this man".

A Deepdene resident recalls seeing the pilot descending in his parachute against a background of flames. It seemed as if he must be engulfed in them. However, he landed in the roadside only slightly hurt.

A tree on the East side of the road was so burnt that it had to be destroyed, although the place where it stood is still visible by a bulge in the pathway. On the West side another flaming tree was saved by pruning and was only felled some 40 years later. (E.O.M.).

<u>April 27/45</u> Review of War Years.

The Dorking Horley Rural Council distributed 1,908 Morrison shelters, 1,750 free and 158 sold. The Government evacuation scheme assumed large proportions in the early war years. During 1939-40, about 500 persons weie received into this district from London and billeted. Excellent work was done by the W.V.S., billeting officers and other voluntary workers. Evacuees now in the district number 483, of whom 89 were unaccompanied children.

<u>May 11/45</u> Civil Defence thanked. Official disbanding in Dorking. Assembling at Pippbrook on Monday evening appropriately within an hour of the announcement of the end of hostilities in Europe. The heads of the Civil Defence Services in the Dorking Urban District received the official thanks of the town for their faithful work throughout the war. The meeting marked the disbanding of Civil Defence.

<u>May 11/45</u> V for Victory. Dorking Celebrates Gaily.

A week's fair on the Dene. Celebrating V.E.Day. Dorking has been en fete this week. Luckily this is the week of Dorking Fair. The caravans and other paraphernalia of the Fair began to arrive on Cotmandene early on Monday, and by Tuesday was for the most part ready for business. The Fair is a statutory fair held annually on Ascension Day (Thursday) and the preceding day. Much as the showmen have wished in the past for an extension of the Fair period, extensions have not been permitted. However the Fair was just the right thing for Victory celebrations - ready-made jollifications, so to speak - and the Dorking Council, as Lords of the Manor of Cotmandene, permitted the Fair to open on Tuesday afternoon, and to remain until tomorrow (Saturday) evening. As an acknowledgement, the showmen are giving £80, which will be divided among the same local charities as the Sunday cinema profits.

Each day from Tuesday until late at night Cotmandene has been crowded with people enjoying all the fun of the Fair. They have been very happy crowds. And there, and elsewhere throughout the district, they have been orderly crowds, and noisy, but the exuberance of their spirits did not lead to excesses.

Red, White and Blue everywhere. On Monday afternoon, while the news of surrender was being awaited, flags and bunting began to appear and, by Tuesday morning, every building carried something in red, white and blue. Most of the flags were not perfectly clean. They, like the people, were showing the signs of a patient perseverance to victory through over five years of war. Still they were victory flags. Every street carried bright festoons. And the people too, adorned themselves with red, white and blue. Tuesday, indeed produced a new feminine fashion - hatless girls all wore red, white and blue hair ribbons. They - the girls as well as the ribbon - were charming.

Dorking's main streets became crowded as Tuesday morning wore on. Steadily the holiday spirit gained vigour until everyone was in high spirits. The tension of five and a half years of war was relaxed. Thankfulness was in everyone's heart. The milk of human friendship flowed to make strangers dance together in the streets as friends. Thanksgiving to God.

As thankfulness is the first thought of this historic V.E.Day, our first record must be of a thanksgiving service at the grand old Church of St.Martin's, the Parish Church of Dorking. Joyful peals of bells called a large congregation to the Church to say prayers of thankfulness and to sing hymns of thankfulness.

"This is an awe-inspiring day" said the Vicar in a brief address. "God has brought us through the long years of darkness, danger and destruction. He has brought us to victory. There is in every heart an inexpressible relief. But thanksgiving is more than that. If that were all, we could go out and give vent to our feelings in unrestrained jubilation. None of us feels we can do just that. It would not be thanksgiving. Thanksgiving means that we recognise and acknowledge that the blessings we have received are a personal gift from God".

Many of the public jollifications were spontaneously arranged and privately organised. A delightful example occurred in Nower Road on Tuesday. Residents there clubbed together most happily. For the children, they arranged races in the roadway, mostly sack races, egg and spoon races, and similar amusing contests. Then, from various houses, tables were produced, set out in the roadway, loaded with food, all provided spontaneously by the good folk of Nower Road, and the children had a grand Victory feast - forgetting rationing for a time. Throughout the evening until late at night, Nower Road continued the festivities with dancing in the roadway and a celebration bonfire.

Dancing in the streets was general. Two big spontaneous

Dorking Church Street party for the home-coming of Mr. Fred Haines who served with the R.A.S.C. in the Middle East. A P.O.W. first in Italy then Germany where he was in the salt mines, they had to walk from camp to mine with ropes round their necks in line, afterwards he never wore a tie. He came home about the end of May and this picture was taken at the home-coming.

dancing parties were in High Street and in West Street. The former was outside S.J. Clear and Co.'s shop where to music amplified through loudspeakers, happy crowds including many Servicemen, danced merrily on the concrete roadway. The forecourt of the Fire station in West Street, together with the roadway, made the other chief alfresco dance hall. There the music for Tuesday night's dance was amplified from Messrs. Gilliam's premises through Michael Gilliam's sound equipment.

For the final death blow of the blackout regulations, there were bonfires everywhere, many buildings showed peace-time lights, and the Northern horizon glowed with the lights of London amid which, around midnight, the searchlights, of evil memory, played victoriously.
Bonfire against Abinger's ruined Church. A notable bonfire, because of its setting, was that at Abinger. The bonfire was built on the Common in front of the ruined Abinger Church destroyed by a flying bomb. The lighting of that fire was done ceremoniously. Service men paraded at 10 p.m. on Tuesday and joined by all the village folk and headed by a mock band, they marched, singing as they marched, in a torchlight procession to the bonfire. There, in a circle of blazing torches, the Rector of Abinger (the Rev. L. Meade) and Canon Parsons conducted a brief service of thanksgiving, and then the fire was lit. The razed walls of the once lovely Norman Church were proudly silhouetted against the blaze of a victory fire. Around the fire, the troops and the civilians joined in the revelry until after midnight.

There were bonfires too, in all other villages. Brockham had a grand bonfire dance on the Green.

Music was played in the Pippbrook grounds. The Prime Minister's announcement and the King's speech on Tuesday were publicly broadcast to the people assembled in various parts of the town.

On Sunday afternoon next, there will be a parade through Dorking of the Civil Defence Services, Police, National Fire Service, Red Cross Society, St.John's Ambulance Brigade, Youth organisations and other uniformed bodies, followed at 3 p.m. by a service of thanksgiving in the grounds of Pippbrook.

<u>May 11/45</u> When an R.A.F. plane crashed at night on Dorking by-pass road last month, doing scarcely any damage, the four members of the crew escaped by parachute. The pilot was the only one injured. He remained at the controls until the last possible moment, gallantly and successfully manoeuvring the plane to prevent it falling on houses. Residents of many houses in the neighbourhood felt they had had a providential escape, and there was heartfelt gratitude to that brave pilot. Barbara Worsfold, aged 14, who lives in Marlborough Road, wished to give practical expression to that gratitude, so she collected money from neighbours to send a gift of cigarettes to the plane's crew. Her mother has now received an acknowledgement from the pilot, Flight

Westcott, Watson Road V.E. day street party.

See page 120

119

Lieut. D.B. Webb. Writing from an R.A.F. hospital he says: "On behalf of the crew and myself, may I convey our most sincere thanks for your very much appreciated gift of cigarettes. It was indeed a wonderful thought of you and your friends, and it took us so completely by surprise that we can hardly find words enough to thank you adequately for your kindness. Indeed, the great help I received after my "arrival" and the excellent attention at your hospital leave me with very pleasant memories of Dorking. You may be interested to know that the crew are safe and well, and that I myself sustained four broken bones in the left foot, so that, apart from suffering the inconvenience of crutches, it is only a matter of time before I, too, will be fit again". The other members of the crew of the plane are given by Flight Lieut. Webb as: Flight Lieut. Watson-Smyth (navigator). Flying Officer Smith (wireless operator), and W.O. Gough (rear gunner).

May 18/45 More Victory celebrations - at Westcott. Westcott's celebration of the great victory culminated in a very happy event on V.E. Day plus one. Taking advantage of the natural arena on Westcott Common, the 17th Dorking (Westcott) Boy Scouts, went to work and organised the show. First the great bonfire was built. On a base 12ft. square it towered up to a good 20ft. at the apex.

Next, the arena was roped off to make the dancing green, and the stage set up, backed by the flag pole. The scouts worked like Trojans and finished well in time.

Lieut. Col. R.W.Barclay spoke of the real purpose of the celebration, reminding all the children that in years to come they must remember not only the bonfire, but rather the great victory. Britain, with her Allies, had won over the foul power of Nazi aggression. It was, he said, a great achievement - unconditional surrender of Germany's might, but the job was not finished yet and they must all work until the Japs, too, are vanquished.

The gaiety continued until midnight finishing up with the crowd dancing and singing round the last great pile of glowing embers, and then home with many a pause to watch the marvellous display of searchlights weaving fantastic patterns over London's sky a last reminder of what this peace means to this country of ours which has endured so much.

May 25/45 More Victory Celebrations. Street Tea dances at Dorking. Lyons Court and Marlborough Road, Orchard Road, Church Gardens, Mount Street, Box Hill.

For the Victory celebrations in Watson Road, Westcott, gaily decorated tables were arranged in the roadway not far from the site occupied by four houses which were demolished, with several fatal casualties by a bomb. The flags of the Allies made a brave Victory reply to that tragedy. The celebrations were organised by Mr. and Mrs. Brown and a committee of helpers. A generous tea was laid out and about 80 children and some parents sat down to a real pre-war feast, Grace and prayers of thanksgiving were said by the Rev. Edwin Tully. Singing and dancing followed. Races

120

were arranged, the winners receiving prizes of Savings Stamps. At 8 o'clock, the children had another round of fruit, cake and soft drinks. Then singing and dancing continued until 11.45 p.m. when everyone present, and there was now a grand party of about 300 - joined hands and sang "Auld Lang Syne", and passed a vote of thanks to Mr. and Mrs. Brown. With cheering and the National Anthem, the party ended at midnight.

June 1/45 V.E. Celebrations. A great day at Capel - in Spring and Curtis Gardens, Bentsbrook Road, North Holmwood. In Cleardene. Bailey Road becomes Lambeth Walk.

About 110 children had a glorious jollification at the Victory party in Bailey Road, Westcott, and the adults , too, found plenty of fun to make the day memorable. First, there was a big

Eastern Command Home Guard.

Sergeant A. Rose.

7th Surrey Battalion.

Your name has been brought to my notice.

I am authorised to signify by the award to you of this Certificate my appreciation of the good service which you have rendered.

I have given instructions that a note of your devotion to duty shall be made on your Record of Service.

Cunningham

Lieutenant-General
General Officer Commanding-in-Chief
Eastern Command.

Date 1st January 1945

Certificate of good service awarded to Sergeant A. Rose. See page 112

Westcott, Bailey Road V.E. day street party

See page 121

tea party in the roadway, most of the food coming from the Bailey Road houses. Then came games and races for the children, with prizes for the winners, and afterwards dancing for all, adults and children. Two London evacuees living in the road gave "turns". One was especially popular. He started the dancers on the Lambeth Walk, and quickly converted Bailey Road into that famous London street. The party was excellently organised by Mrs. Bartlett. A sum of £23.10s was collected. Of that, £11 remains. This is going towards a fund to give the children of Westcott an August outing to the seaside.

June 8/45 Fairfield Drive, Church Street, Mid and South Holmwood had Victory teas.

June 15/45 Westcott Civil Defence entertained. The First Aid Party, Rescue Party and wardens of Westcott were hospitably entertained by Mrs. Donovan Touche, at a farewell party on Wednesday last week. The weather was unkind, but a pause between the showers enabled the guests to see the attractive garden. Refreshments were served on a generous scale, and the gathering enabled those who had spent many anxious hours together during the past six years to renew their friendship in happier circumstances. At the end of the evening the Head Warden (Mr. W. Etheridge) expressed briefly, but with great sincerity the gratitude of the company, who, to show their approval of his speech, informed their hostess with uplifted voices that "She was a jolly good fellow".

June 15/45 Ranmore Home Guard. Last of the Stand Down Dinners.

June 29/45 Home Guard Shooting. Twenty six members of the Dorking Home Guard Rifle Club went to the Westcott Range on Saturday afternoon, and favoured by excellent weather, had a very enjoyable shoot. The scores obtained were quite good, on taking into consideration the rifles used are fitted with open sights,and the winning score of G.H. May, who obtained 40 out of a possible 50, was excellent. The next Club shoot takes place also at Westcott Range, on Sunday July 8th and is an all day shoot.

August 17/45 Complete Victory. V.J. jollifications in Dorking. Jubilant crowds everywhere.

The pealing of bells and the firing of fireworks in the first hour of Wednesday morning, awakened many Dorking people to tell them that Japan had surrendered, and that the world was free once again of war.

Some Dorking people did not need to be awakened by bells and fireworks to learn the glad news. They had waited for the midnight radio announcement, and they quickly let their neighbours know! Thus ended those anxious days while the world wondered whether Japan would accept unconditional surrender.

Soon after breakfast time on Wednesday, Dorking began to assume the gay dress of V.J. Day. The flags and bunting put away since V.E. Day came out again. As the day wore on, the main streets became brightly festooned with flag and bunting decorations, and few houses ended the day without some visible expression of the joy of victory.

However, the first pre-occupation of most housewives was shopping. Larders had to be stocked, within the limits of rationing, and short supplies, for two days' holiday. By 9 a.m. Dorking's High Street was crowded with shoppers. Queues were bigger than normally. But on this day at least the shoppers were patient and good tempered, and well laden baskets were going homewards by midday. After that the town went into a holiday mood.

Dancing round the Bandstand. The chief night jollifications were centred round the bandstand in South Street. The bandstand and the railings along the high road above the bandstand were festooned with bunting and coloured electric lights. Microphones were installed on the bandstand. A party of men had obviously been very busy on the instructions of the Urban District Council - and Dorking thanks the Council and the men for their speedy and effective work. The Council had arranged for two bands - Gordon Bishop's augmented by Vic Luff's and then the Metric Dance Band - to play in turn at the bandstand for dancing.

Soon after 8 p.m. dancing began. It continued until the next morning. There were a few interruptions, but these were exciting and welcome interruptions, small scale firework displays, consisting chiefly of flares, which made terrific glows for long periods. At the height of the dancing there must have been five thousand people around the bandstand. The crowd was gay but admirably behaved. Servicemen were prominent among the revellers.

A novelty - or it seems a novelty, excepting to those with long memories - made the V.J. Day memorable. All the street lights were on! Arranging this had made J.E.A. men busy, but they managed it, and Dorking is grateful even though full street lighting may not yet be a permanency.

Of course there were celebrations in side streets as well as in the main streets. These were chiefly in the form of bonfires and fireworks.

An hour's extension was granted on V.J. Day. The Victory celebrations continued yesterday (Thursday). The Urban Council arranged for a repetition of the dancing in South Street around the bandstand, outside the Fire station, and possibly at the Odd Fellows' Hall. In case of wet weather the Drill Hall was booked.

The villages throughout the Dorking area had their Victory celebrations also with smaller crowds, there was gay dancing in the Street at Capel on Wednesday evening, and impromptu sports

124

and a fete were arranged to take place in the Recreation ground.

August 24/45 V.J. Days. Dorking celebrations continued. A few street parties on Wednesday. Falkland Road, Falkland Hill, Hampstead Road and Harrowgate Gardens, Overdale, Capel, Brockham Green.

The re-introduction of street lighting in Dorking, now to be on every night, has shown that during the six years of war, trees and hedges have in several places grown so much as to obscure much of the light from the lamps.

September 7/45 Westcott a Victory party.

Excellent co-operation and generous suport ensured the success of a V.J. celebration party for the residents of Watson Road, Ashley Road and part of Furlong Road. Mr. and Mrs. Brown organised the party, which started with a procession of children in fancy dress, from the bomb damaged shelter in Watson Road. The procession moved to the Hut for tea, Mr. Sheppard leading and ringing the "All Clear". At the Hut, a gorgeous tea party began with a welcome by Mrs. Brown, and grace said by the Rev. E. Tully, of St.John's Church. The party began amid laughter as Mr. Whitelock walked in dressed as a "Nippy" to wait on the children, and laughter was the keynote of the merry evening that followed. For late workers, there was a late tea, and everyone had supper at 8.30 p.m. After that, adults enjoyed dancing for an hour and a half, and then came community singing. A Welsh anthem was sung as a duet in Welsh by Mrs. Woods and Mrs. Lloyd. The happy party ended with all singing, and after, a minute's silence in memory of the fallen, the National Anthem.

This next party is included for the benefit of John Coombes who remembers it well.

September 7/45 A Victory party for Dene Street area. A grand time was had by all, both young and old, on Thursday, when Dene Street and Dene Street Gardens held their V.J. party. Great activity was noticed in Dene Street at about 3.15 p.m., where a crowd of youngsters, a number in fancy dress gathered in readiness to proceed to the Odd Fellows' Hall, where a glorious spread of pre-war quality awaited them. The Rev. A.C. Nickol kindly attended and said Grace, after which about 80 children did their best to spoil the look of trifles, jellies, blancmanges, sandwiches, sponge cakes, numerous fancy cakes, and finally a portion of an iced Victory cake.

Tea over, next came the fancy dress competition. An exceptionally good show of costumes made judging very difficult. First prize was awarded to a toddler, Alan Knight, in a very original costume, "Is this the New World", second prize went to Linda Croft, who represented "Cupid 1945" and third prize winners were Frank and Ruth Goldsmith, "Darby and Joan". Mr. Sydney Croft, who was in charge of the entertainment, then announced

Cpl. Reed, of the R.A.S.C. who played the piano.

The talent competition brought the future variety stars to the stage. This was won by two youngsters with a duet, "You are my sunshine", sung by Veronica Frazer and Judy Harris. Second and third place were also taken by duets sung by Josephine Smith and Margaret Gill, and Sheila Stoner and Ann Davis. Following this, all the children had an opportunity to display their talent in a glorious sing-song led by Cpl. Reed and "Uncle Sid". Then came the great moment for the older children, the appearance of the conjurer (Mr. Edgar Stevens), who gave them an hour's entertainment. Following this, "Uncle Ted" introduced Councillor Bell, who kindly came along and had a few words with the children. Each child then received half a crown, an apple and sweets. Three rousing cheers were given for Councillor Bell and all helpers and people responsible for such a grand time that was enjoyed by all. A social and dance was arranged for the older generation. Dancing continued until refreshments were served. This was followed by an hours excellent entertainment by local artists who kindly came along. Miss Audrey Knowles, whose excellent singing is well known locally, opened the programme, accompanied by Mr. George Osborne at the piano, Jack Clarke entertained with his accordion and jokes, followed by a spot of community singing enjoyed by all, and finally songs by Miss T. Croft and Miss G. Longhurst. Dancing continued with a waltz competition, judged by the Croft brothers, the winners being Miss Wareham and partner first, and Miss G. Longhurst and partner second. Another prize was won by Miss Harrison.

Dancing continued until 11.30. A grand time was enjoyed by all, made possible by the generosity of residents in Dene Street and Dene Street Gardens and hard work enjoyably carried out by the committee and Mr. S. Croft.

September 14/45 Cotmandene V.J. party on Thursday last week.

September 21/45 Westcott Celebrates Victory. Westcott's turn in Victory celebrations came on Wednesday. They had a fine day, sandwiched marvellously between some unpleasantly wet days.

First the children, many in fancy costume, assembled at the Hut, and a carnival paraded around the village to the Belmont School playing field.

Fun on the Heath. Around 7 p.m. all Westcott went to the Heath for further festivities. Here there was a lively concert run in an informal way under the directions of Mr. W. Glass. Mrs. Lloyd and Mr. H. Brinkworth sang songs.

Then came a grand display of fireworks given by Capt. Schermuly and Mr. A.G. Palmer.

The Victory bonfire followed. It was an impressive sight when, after a torchlight procession, the torchbearers (Boy Scouts) formed a Victory V and then, with their torches, lit the bonfire

126

to start a great blaze which quickly consumed the Japanese flag surmounting the bonfire.

September 21/45 After five years of excellent work, the "Stand Easy" canteen for the Forces, in West Street, Dorking, closed on Saturday last. Established in June 1940, the "Stand Easy" has been opened every evening including Sundays, holidays and Christmas Days, becoming a bright and busy spot in the town's war activities. It was popular with all branches of the Services, mainly because of the excellent refreshments supplied at very low prices and the atmosphere of friendliness and informality. The canteen was run on a voluntary basis by a happy company of ladies, who saw to it that all visitors were made welcome. Throughout the five years, these amateur waitresses have cheerfully given their time and labour to put a touch of comfort into the lives of troops who were training in the area. In addition to serving members of the armed Forces, the "Stand Easy" was of inestimable value on several nights during the blitz period in supplying meals to part time N.F.S. men before they set out on long night journeys to raided towns. All who helped in the canteen's success are thanked, including those who gave or lent furniture and books.

November 23/45 War Exhibitions in Dorking's Thanksgiving Week. Thanksgiving week brought three very interesting exhibitions to Dorking. All were concerned with various aspects of Britains war effort and illustrated vividly how some of the money invested in National Savings was spent by the Government to help our Forces win a great Victory.

Throughout the week, from Monday onwards, a Thanksgiving and local war work exhibition has been staged in the Martineau Hall at Dorking Halls. This by the way, is the first time Dorking Halls have been used by the public since September, 1939, when they were requisitioned for war purposes.

Around two sides of the Martineau Hall and overflowing into the corridors were arranged illuminated cases illustrating with diagrams and models, Britain at War and Britain preparing for reconstruction after victory. This was the official Thanksgiving exhibition in charge of two soldiers. Allied with that, and occupying most of the floor space, were examples of the many and varied munitions of war made in the Dorking area since 1939. The display was a startling "eye opener". Scarcely a person in Dorking could have known that such a wide variety of articles used in war was being manufactured here, and no one knew the production figures. The exhibition revealed much of this was secret and the revelation was astounding. Furthermore, the display of local war work was a valuable object lesson, illustrating the usefulness of dispersal into small factories. Altogether, the exhibition was an admirably appropriate event for Thanksgiving Week.

The exhibitors' stands are reviewed below in alphabetical order.

E.J. Baker and Co: showed a big selection of parts of war's implements, many complicated and demanding the utmost precision. Their production figures were impressive - aircraft components, 203,648: gun components, 130,487. And many of those components were not small, simple affairs. For example, there were elevating gears for heavy guns, mountings for the 6 pounder and 17 pounder, tank gun, and bases for the Bofors turntable. Examples were shown of the firm's prototype war work. These were strangely shaped pieces of dural metal (an aluminium alloy) cut from big blocks, the work being done in absolute precision for experimental planes.

S.J. Clear and Co: normally radio and electrical engineers, turned over to war work in addition to continuing their normal business. They made 4,500 electrical switchboxes for auto-gyro compasses, over a quarter million nuts for Bren gun carriers and tanks, 30,000 cartridge containers for the 4.2 in. mortar, 10,000 lampholder sets and 25,000 shell fuse cap rings. The switchbox was a maze of pieces of metal, yet it was assembled by women who, before the war, had scarcely ever used a screwdriver. The lampholder set was a life saving device for a light to float on the sea after a ship had been sunk.

Dorking Foundry Ltd: were engaged mainly on the production of iron castings and machine tools. Their output included 880 motor driven hacksawing machines, 300 fly presses and 2,400 machine vices. They made a total of 4,246 machine tools comprising 150,000 parts, and about 300,000 screwed bomb nose adaptors. Their exhibit included several big and complicated machine tools.

Dorking Motor Co : showed the production methods by which workers there produced nearly two million Bofors shell cases and a quarter million cartridge containers for mortars. For the shell cases, there were 33 operations before the finished article was reached. The average number of work people engaged was 100, half of whom were women and all unskilled when they began. Their peak production of shell cases for a week was 15,603. In addition, the company made 3,674 aero tent sockets, 4,269 welded fly nuts and many other things for the war machine. Also, as exhibited on their stand, they ingeniously repaired old valves and turned them out as new.

Moss Bros: War work of a different sort was displayed by Moss Bros, the clothiers. Their stand exhibited specimens of the uniforms for the Services produced from their Dorking factory. They made 103,800 garments during the war.

H.R. Nash Ltd: rebuilt 9,200 Service motor cycles between 1941 and 1945. Their chief exhibits were a badly crashed motor cycle, looking an almost hopeless wreck and, against it, a motor cycle which had been rebuilt with all its broken parts replaced or repaired. Also shown were specimens of clean and shining engines which had been reconditioned mostly by women. That must have been greasy difficult work. They did it admirably and happily.

Pneumatic Tent Co: war work was largely associated with the R.A.F., but not entirely. Employing many women, they produced during the war over 500,000 items, used 5,000 miles of fabric, 1,000 miles of cordage and over three million eyelets. They produced 30,000 aircraft shelters, 230 rubber dinghies, 20,000 weather covers, 30,000 aircraft wheel covers, 2,400 supply dropping parachutes, 20,000 flare dropping parachutes, 16,250 cases for carrying rubber boats or portable aerials through jungle country, 33,000 distress signal flags, and 6,000 sails for emergency dinghies (the sails bearing printed operational instructions for the airmen forced to become sailors), and they repaired 10,000 R.A.F. tool boxes. The exhibition of specimens of the many R.A.F. supplies produced by the Pneumatic Tent Co, attracted a lot of attention.

Road Plant Construction Co: was engaged in manufacturing snow ploughs, massive affairs used for clearing roadways and airfield runways; gritting and salt spreading machines to make runways usable in frosty weather; ventilators for ships; explosion vessels for depth charge throwers; electric furnaces for annealing (hardening) parts of aero engines; components of mechanical sweepers used for sweeping runways; and cutting augers for boring holes for explosive charges. Examples of several of those strange appliances were shown.

The S.P.R.A. Co: many wonderful gadgets were shown in the war work display by the Schermuly Pistol Rocket Apparatus Co. This company made life saving apparatus in peace time and much of its war work was similarly concerned with life saving, but not entirely. They showed a route marking bomb carried by the Pathfinders. Of this bomb, each containing 27 flares, they made 3,500. They made half a million rockets which sent up a cable attached to a parachute. They made thousands of rockets which were fired from ships to light up the sea's surface when U-boats were suspected. They made three and a half million target identification flares used in concentrated bombing and 425,000 reconnaissance flares. Of buoyant rockets and lines for airborne lifeboats they made 20,000, and 10 million R.A.F. recognition signal cartridges. One of their ingenious productions was a rocket which took up a kite. The action of the wind on the kite pulled up an aerial so that airmen in a dinghy could send radio messages. Among the rockets made, also used in peacetime, were those used by sea planes to illuminate the surface of water on which they wished to descend so that the pilots can see there are no obstacles.

Sherlock and Sons: Welding was the chief war work by Sherlock and Sons, and it was done in a big way, as their exhibits showed. The main exhibit was the base assembly and towing appliance for a 4.2 in. mortar. The firm were responsible for the whole of the fabricating and welding of 600 of these heavy chassis. They also made 4,000 of the complete base (designed by them) for the 3 in . mortar. Another of their exhibits was a 90 gallon auxiliary petrol tank carried by fighters to increase their range. This tank carried also a grenade so that when jettisoned with a few gallons remaining in it, it became a nasty fire bomb. Sometimes the full tank was jettisoned. Sherlock and Sons also made bomb slings for loading 1,000 lb. bombs on to Typhoons and similar aircraft and a complicated balancing gear for howitzers.

November 30/45   Dorking Council. A bit of old Dorking lost. The Highways Committee received a letter from the Dorking and Leith Hill District Preservation Society regarding the old sign post removed from the pump at the Pump Corner in the early days of the war. The Surveyor stated that this and other signs were taken to the depot and instructions were given that they should be kept in a safe place. The sign taken from the pump could not now be found. The Surveyor submitted a sketch of the proposed new sign.

"There are enough obstacles on Pump Corner now", said Mr. Woodward. "It is a veritable nightmare to get round that corner".

Miss Evans regretted the loss of the sign post,a piece of Dorking's history.

Mr. Hatswell: "I have not given up hope that it may still turn up somewhere in our depot".

                    *   *   *

January 25/46   Men of the 1st. Battalion of the Hastings and Prince Edward Regiment, Ontario, Canada, retain happy memories of Reigate, Betchworth and Dorking. Attached to the First Canadian Division, they were billeted in the Betchworth district during the greater part of 1940. They were given a great reception on their return to the homeland, and the Picton "Times" Ontario, published a special profusely illustrated number in their honour. Some of the most interesting pictures were taken at Reigate. They depict the Battalion parading to Church services which were held in Surrey towns and villages, and the Battalion "with heads bowed in prayer". Says the chronicler, "A most impressive sight. Add to this the green hills of Surrey and you have an extravaganza, a setting of reverence to behold". There is a picture of two of these warriors from overseas at a piano brought along to help in the singing of the services. "These are scenes", it is recorded, "the remaining originals are familiar with, and will help to renew memories of Reigate and its many beauties". The men of this Battalion proudly carried the famous Patch of the First Division on active service and won many battle honours in the compaigns in Sicily, where they fought on the beaches and in Italy.

For details of this Regiment see: "Duffy's Regiment": a History of the Hastings and Prince Edward Regiment, by Kenneth B. Smith. 1987.

February 22/46   Dorking Bench. "Will ye no come back again".

The Court list contained the names of two Canadian soldiers summoned for committing damage to a telephone kiosk in Horsham Road, Dorking. Reporting that the two men had been repatriated to Canada, Supt. Hilton said it was useless to adjourn the summonses, and he added;"It only means waiting on until there is another war and they return to this country." The summonses were withdrawn.

March 29/46 Dorking Urban Council. Parish Pump Politics. To the Highway Committee, the Surveyor presented a drawing taken from photographs in the possession of the Surrey Archaeological Society and submitted by the Dorking and Leith Hill Preservation Society showing the direction sign at Pump Corner as it was originally.

The committee decided to erect an exact copy of the sign and also to erect an independent advance direction sign.

Major Chance objected to dance and other advertisements being placed on the pump.

The Chairman: To whom does the pump belong?

Major Chance: The pump is public and can be used by the inhabitants at large. The question of whether the few stones around it are private property was the subject of a dispute which I do not think has been settled.

The Council went on to discuss the proposed sign. Some doubt was expressed as to whether it would be an exact replica of the old sign. Several councillors regarded the sign, not being on the left hand side of the road, as almost useless for motorists, and they contended that, if an exact replica of the old sign could not be assured, it would be better to fix a modern sign. However, the committee's report was accepted.

April 12/46 Abinger Ammunition Dump.

In the House of Commons last week, Mr. Wilson Harris (a resident of Abinger) asked the Secretary of State for War, when the ammunition dump at Abinger, which was to have been cleared by March 31st, will in fact be cleared.

Mr. Lawson replied: "All ammunition, apart from smoke generators, has been cleared from this area. The disposal of the smoke generators by burning or dumping at sea has been delayed by weather conditions. Efforts to complete the clearance at the earliest possible date will continue to be made".

April 19/46 Dorking Toc H Club. End of a fine piece of war work. The Dorking Toc H Services Club in High Street will close on Saturday, April 20th, there being now very few troops stationed in this area. Thus will end a magnificent piece of voluntary service for the welfare of men and women in khaki, naval and Air Force blue, not forgetting also the brown and green of the Women's Land Army.

At the Club throughout six years has been done by a small body of men and women a volume of work the extent of which very few of the public can have realised. Military censorship forbade any Press reference to the Club during the war, so there was none of the lime light of publicity to show the public what was being done for the comfort of local Service folk. Yet the Club became well known and extremely popular among the thousands of Service men and women who, at various times, came into camps and billets in this district. At its busiest period the Club was providing four to five hundred meals each evening - sausage and chips, with bread and butter and a cup of tea was the favourite - as well as providing a comfortable haven in which the men and women could write their letters, read, play games or listen to music.

Running the Club, preparing the meals, serving, washing up and all the other jobs made a tremendous call upon the time and energy of the small body of Toc H helpers, but with splendid self sacrifice they stuck to their self imposed job. There were women who were kept hard at it cooking chip potatoes,for example, from 6 p.m. to 10 p.m. That job, particularly in the summer months, must have been exhausting. As the war proceeded, the male workers become fewer in numbers through young Toc H members being called to the Forces. So those left behind had to do a bit more until they were spending two or three evenings a week, from 5.30 to 10 p.m., going hard at it at the Club. These men, in addition to their ordinary work, shared also in civil defence duties.

The Club had a small beginning. In the early days of the war the local branch of Toc H opened their own headquarters in Chart Lane as a meeting place for evacuated children and their parents. Soon arose the necessity to do something for soldiers being drafted into the area. As the number of troops increased the old headquarters became inadequate and the branch committee looked for more suitable premises. These were found in the old Dorking Club rooms in High Street. The owner, Mrs. Lloyd, kindly allowed Toc H to use the premises as a club for the duration of the war rent free. This was a fine beginning, and the members set to with a great heart to put the rooms into suitable condition. In May 1940, the Club was opened. Later when the premises passed into the ownership of Meux's Breweries, the same kindly consideration of freedom from rent was continued.

The Army welfare department soon asked the Toc H branch to take over the "A" licence for the area. This meant that instead of devoting the Club chiefly to the recreational needs of the Forces it became mainly a canteen. A rota of some 50 lady helpers was put into operation, and as the Toc H men were gradually absorbed into the Forces themselves the work fell increasingly on the ladies, aided by the few remaining men. The Club premises consisted of a large games room with two billiards tables and table tennis, a reading and writing room, and a canteen and kitchen. It was open daily from 5.30 p.m. to 10 p.m., and on Saturday and Sunday afternoons from 2.30 p.m.

All through the war six women and one man were on duty every night. Concerts under the personal direction of Dr. Vaughan Williams were given as an experiment each week for the year 1941-42, and each year until 1945 a Christmas party was given. The concerts had to be abandoned as the premises were not suitable for accommodating both a concert audience and the crowds of troops clamouring to be served at the canteen.

During the six years' life of the canteen about a million hot beverages and nearly the same total of meals were served. That is a fine record of unselfish sacrifice by those who gave their time and energies to a grand piece of work. Although the meals were sold at cost price - 7d. was the price of the normal supper of sausage and chips, bread and butter and tea, and no effort was made to run at a profit, the canteen was self supporting.

June 7/46 Dorking W.V.S., in consultation with the Urban Council, have decided the time has come for them to give up their office at Pippbrook. They do this with regret after seven years of what they believe to have been useful work; and wish to express their sincere thanks to all their members and to the people of Dorking and district who, by their help and sympathy, have enabled work which at times seemed almost insurmountable to be carried through successfully.

October 11/46 Homeless move to Bury Hill Army huts. There are 29 huts altogether, but two of them were severely damaged by a falling tree.

December 29/1950 The Ministry of Works is to be told that the Bury Hill huts vacated by tenants now rehoused by the Council are no longer required by the Council.

August 14/1953 Extract from a letter:"When will the derelict hut site at Bury Hill be cleaned up and a few trees planted at the Nower to succeed those now decaying?"

The Deepdene, Dorking was the Southern Railway's war time headquarters. See:"War on the Line". The Southern Railway in wartime by Bernard Darwin 1946.

The Dorking and District Refugee Committee was inaugurated on 1st December 1938, and now after eleven years its work has come to an end.

The first refugees to be cared for by the Committee were from Czechoslovakia; it is believed that these were the first Sudeten - Czechs to reach this country in their efforts to escape imprisonment and probably death. Within six months of their arrival a party of some forty of these had emigrated to British Columbia. To prepare them for the new life some men had had agricultural training on farms in the district, and others lessons in shoe repairing. The early outbreak of war put a stop to any further large scale emigration.

The Czech refugees were soon joined by Jewish refugees from Central Europe. Up to the outbreak of war the Committee were deeply concerned with efforts to get children of Jewish origin or whose family were "suspect" into England. The success of these efforts was due to the sympathy of those who offered homes to these children adopting them into their families. Other children came over with their mothers, for whom the Committee found domestic posts, thus ensuring to both mother and child a safe asylum. In addition many children who came to England through other agencies were cared for by this Committee. These children are now started in life, either in this country, or in Palestine or elsewhere, and are making their contribution to the life of the community.

The Committee would express its very sincere thanks to those who lent or rented houses as hostels for the homeless refugees who came to Dorking; without their generous aid the work of the Committee would have come to an untimely end.

The first party of refugees was housed at Fairhaven, the Bermondsey Settlement Camp at Holmbury St.Mary, for which a nominal rent was paid, but this camp was not available during the summer months, and in March 1939 the refugees moved to Somerset Hill, which was lent by Dame Edith Lyttleton for three months. There they were joined by a party from Clarendon House, which hostel had for three months been entirely run, equipped and financed by the Dorking Congregational Church.

When the three months' tenancy of Somerset Hill ended the Duke of Newcastle let the Committee have Burchett House rent free as a Refugee Hostel. After his death the Newcastle Estates Ltd, generously allowed the tenancy to continue on the same terms, and Burchett House was"home" to many refugees for a period of rather more than ten years.

Warren Farm in Tillingbourne Valley was let furnished to the Committee by Mrs. Lloyd, and provided a home for ten Sudetens from September 1939 to June 1941.

In all some 130 people (47 single folk and 30 families) passed through Burchett House during the Committee's tenancy, the length of stay varying from two days to over nine years. In addition to these the Committee has been in touch with and given help to many refugees resident in the district.

Where are all these people now? Has the work attempted by the Committee been worth doing?

Some qualified refugee doctors are working in hospitals in this country, others are employed in engineering and agricultural work. During the war several Czech refugees served in the Pioneer Corps of the army, and at the end of hostilities many of the younger Jewish men and women went as interpreters to the U.S.A. Army of Occupation in Germany. Quite a few of these young women did not return to England but went direct to U.S.A. as the wives of American soldiers.

Some of our friends, after long delay, have emigrated to the U.S.A, to Canada and to South America. Some have returned to help in the rebuilding of their own national life, and many have become naturalised and settled in this country.

Mention has been made in former reports of the outstanding successes of some "child" refugees in the scholastic world. Perhaps a good way to end this article would be by quoting a letter received in September last from one of our refugees who, after being employed for some years on different farms in this district, has now a farm of his own. He writes: "We are getting on very well here and have become successful. Our land yields the highest crops round here, though the land on our farm had been derelict for all the time before, and known as not worth being farmed. We started with one cow, at present we have eight, and I am shortly to buy another six. My wife has become very used to her job, better than I ever expected. She has to help milking, and she cares for over 200 chicken with great enthusiasm.

In the meantime we have become naturalised too".

But the final word in this report must be one of great appreciation of, and hearty thanks for the many services rendered by the great body of Friends of Dorking Refugees who have helped in so many ways in the past eleven years. Only a few of these can be mentioned by name, but our thanks are in a very special way due:

1. To all who offered and gave homes to children.

2. To the medical men, Dr. Dyson and his partners, and the late Dr. Stone, who for years gave their services free of charge.

3. To Lord Green who gave us free legal advice on many of our problems.

4. And to busy men who, as Honorary Treasurers of the Committee, saw that our budget was balanced. Here we would mention by name two of these who are no longer with us, the late Cecil V. Barker, Esq., and the late H. Harper Esq.

END.

ABBREVIATIONS

AFS	Auxiliary Fire Service
ARP	Air Raid Precautions
ATC	Air Training Corps
ATS	Auxiliary Territorial Service
BEF	British Expeditionary Force
DUC	Dorking Urban Council
DUDC	Dorking Urban District Council
HE	High Explosive
JEA	Joint Electricity Authority
LDV	Local Defence Volunteers
NAAFI	Navy, Army and Air Force Institute
NFS	National Fire Service
POW	Prisoner of War
RASC	Royal Army Service Corps
REME	Royal Electrical and Mechanical Engineers
UXB	Unexploded Bomb
VE	Victory in Europe
VJ	Victory over Japan
WI	Women's Institute
WO	Warrant Officer
WVS	Women's Voluntary Service, later the Women's Royal Voluntary Service
YMCA	Young Men's Christian Association